THE VOICE OF JOLIET

THE LIFE AND TIMES OF HALL OF FAME RADIO SPORTSCASTER DON LADAS

by
Gary Seymour

authorHOUSE®

AuthorHouse™ UK Ltd.
500 Avebury Boulevard
Central Milton Keynes, MK9 2BE
www.authorhouse.co.uk
Phone: 08001974150

© 2008 Gary Seymour. All rights reserved.

No part of this book may be reproduced, stored in a retrieval system, or transmitted by any means without the written permission of the author.

First published by AuthorHouse   6/9/2008

ISBN: 978-1-4343-9287-9 (sc)

Printed in the United States of America
Bloomington, Indiana

This book is printed on acid-free paper.

Foreword

The stock answer to the question of how you enjoy covering sports for a living is that it beats working.

Throughout the 14 years I spent in the "toy department" of the Herald News in Joliet, I was assigned to various beats that were greatly rewarding on both a professional and personal level. I sat with Michael Jordan in the locker room at the Delta Center in Salt Lake City, Utah, hours before he stole the ball from Karl Malone to give the Bulls the last of their six championships in that fabulous run of the 1990s.

I saw the 1988 New Year's Eve playoff game at Soldier Field where the Bears beat Philadelphia in an opaque blanket of fog that gave the game a weird-dream quality. Come to think of it, I didn't really see that one. But I did see and write about the White Sox's playoff loss to Toronto in '93, and I was in Seattle when the Mariners knocked the Sox out of the 2000 postseason.

In the '98 playoffs I paid 75 dollars to park in a tiny, pothole-filled lot near Wrigley Field – reimbursed, thankfully – and watched Atlanta turn out the lights on the Cubs' World Series hopes. Ten years before that, I was at the Friendly Confines when the Cubs finally turned *on* the lights. And I covered the best hockey, basketball and baseball players in the world when the all-star games for those sports came to Chicago.

Gratifying as it was to write about the pros, it was in covering the high school, college and youth sports where I cultivated the deepest and most lasting friendships, including that with the protagonist of this book. My journalism career in Joliet had a nice little symmetry to it. The first interview I did at the paper was with Don Ladas, the WJOL radio sportscaster who on that day was pulling together all the particulars for the annual Multiple Sclerosis Benefit Softball Game. He was helpful, patient and friendly – the kind of person you like instantly.

For my last interview in Joliet, I was answering and not asking the questions. Don Ladas had me on his show to talk about things I'd seen and done at the Herald News. He was gracious and encouraging, as he had always been for the 14 years between those two interviews.

Researching this book, I was impressed by a comment made by pitcher Bill Gullickson, who like many Joliet folks I've had the pleasure of meeting is congenial and sincere. Gully said that whenever he was approached by Don, it was an honor for him to give the interview. I felt the same when Don asked me to write about his life.

Rare are the 79-year-olds whose only regret is that there's no longer much giddy-up in their get-along. Don is indeed a rare one, not in that he has demonstrated integrity, courtesy and humility – a lot of people hit that trifecta – but in that he has demonstrated those qualities unceasingly. His generosity is well-known, and his compassion is such that he'd hold an umbrella over a duck in a rain shower.

Being the loyal guy that he is, Don hoped to get WJOL's call letters in the title of this book. But after having spoken with as many people as I did and having so many of them – with no prompting – refer to him as the voice of Joliet, it could not have been called anything else. Besides, the call letters *are* on the front, if you look at it. Like my friend Joe Rodeghero said, "WJOL and Don Ladas are the same word."

The only success in life is to spend it in your own way, and Don has done that. The fact that spending his life in his own way meant that at the same time he was also helping so many people feel good about themselves is all you need to know about him. That's more than a success. That's a whale of a job.

With a heart rate somewhere around 250 and his brow leaking a beady glaze, the nicest guy in the world took a deep breath.

Don Ladas looked over and beyond the black ball he held with both hands in front of him, studying the 10 pins arranged in the triangle 60 feet away, inviting him to open the door to bowling's penthouse and come on in.

The faraway rumble of splattering wood had stopped for a while now, once it had become apparent that Don's bid for a perfect 300 game was a serious one. Everyone at the Elks bowling alley in Joliet, Illinois, had put down their balls, grabbed their drinks and sidled over to check it out.

Don would have preferred they'd stayed where they were. That way it might have been easier to not think about what was happening. His thought-processing circuitry on a normal day was a raging torrent, but with a 300 game in reach the waves of brain activity had become a tsunami. It was getting hard to see straight.

He'd been on fire at the alley before, many times, but never like this. In his previous game in league play that night in 1953 he finished with six straight strikes. Now, with nine more in a row to start this one, it was 15 and counting. He was on the verge of a huge milestone.

A perfect game back then was far more rare than it is today for a couple of reasons, one being that athletes simply get better throughout the passing of time. In 1953 the four-minute-mile barrier was still a year away from being broken.

Another reason the perfect game was more difficult at that time is that the sport was still crawling through early stages of development. Bowling in that era looked more like the game Fred Flintstone played, minus the dinosaurs.

With automatic pin-setting machines not yet on the scene, pins boys were still lurking back in the pits, resetting each new formation by hand. Lane dressing was primitive. Bowling ball covers were made of hard plastic, or, as was the case with the first ball Don used, cork. Modern bowling ball coverstocks are made of urethane, particle and reactive resin, and today there is such emphasis on things like momentum and transferred energy and particles and ratio-of-force that you wonder if bowling ball research is done at Fermilab.

Baseball has been coy about revealing changes in specs designed to give their ball more pop, and thereby ramp up the offensive numbers that create more buzz for their product, but not bowling. Advances in bowling ball technology have been widely heralded.

But bowlers in 1953 weren't throwing a Proton Supercollider 4000. A perfect game rolled with a ball much less physics-friendly was roughly equal to a pitcher today throwing a no-hitter for 10 innings instead of nine.

Maybe even 11 innings, who knows. That sort of abstract rhetoric is the stuff that Don would later embrace as a radio host, but he didn't have that job yet. On that night in '53 he was a sportswriter and a student, a softball player and a league bowler, flirting madly with perfection while a crowd hovered in a half-circle of muted frenzy. Don did his best to pull in all the oxygen he could, and then exhaled, his every move tracked by the spellbound, Hamms-steeped gallery.

In a flawed world inhabited by flawed people, there is something irresistible about perfection in sports competition. Whether it's the lightning-strike beauty of a hole-in-one or the dramatic buildup of a no-hitter, most share in the vicarious thrill of having been on board, in person, for the rare human triumph over long odds. A cynical few delight in seeing a balloon blown up and then busted; envy and jealousy are natural emotions that probably date back to prehistoric squabbles about who discovered fire.

Either way, when something big is happening everyone wants to have a look.

But while it's impossible to know what was on the minds of each person at the Elks that night, it's a fair bet that everyone in the crowd was pulling for Don to close out his gem.

And why not. He'd always been the first guy at the plate waiting to congratulate the teammate finishing his home run trot. He was the one insisting that next time would be different after his bowling team beat yours. And if you ever needed a ride to work or five bucks till next Wednesday, you could always count on his helping hand. Fifteen minutes with Don Ladas is enough to weigh the sincerity of his intent and convince you that if he isn't the nicest guy in the world, then he is no worse than in a first-place tie.

Or maybe he's the luckiest guy in the world.

Here was a man who got a weight-doubling growth spurt *after* he graduated high school, a guy who would go on to enjoy eight decades of almost perfect health, work the job of his fantasy, marry the girl of his dreams and live in a household with three children any parent would be proud to call theirs. He would become a sports radio broadcaster inducted into nine Halls of Fame without having gotten one coach fired, without having uncovered a single scandal and without having registered as much as a 2 on the faultfinding Zing-o-Meter, let alone a 10.

And regardless of the era, a 300 game still requires at least a bit of a cuddle from Lady Luck.

"How I got so hot is something I never could figure out," he said. "Really, I was bowling just naturally. Any time the ball went near the pocket, down they'd go. It's like any sport; you've got to be good, but you also have to be lucky. All I remember is that I was nervous as heck."

For what he would become to the Joliet bowling community, it was a propitious moment. His father opened the first alley in the city, and Don took the baton and ran with it. Don was the guy organizing all the side bets and the pick-up tournaments. He was known at every alley in town, and for Joliet bowlers he would faithfully carry water – and beer – for more than a half-century.

His Ten Pin Topics radio show on WJOL would become the aural wallpaper in the daily landscape of the city, and the country's longest-running bowling broadcast, too. Being there for his first 300 game would be like watching Yoda pull his first spaceship out of the swamp.

So against a backdrop of disquieting silence and three strikes from nirvana, Don took his five-step approach, bent at the knees, reared back and fired.

The energy careening through the alley gave the place a surreal tinge. It took forever for the ball to get there, and its rolling hum seemed louder than usual as it cut a path just right of the center arrow.

Finally, after the interminable, nerve-wracking buildup, it took about eight-tenths of a second for everyone to process the result. He missed the head pin. Nine pins scattered, but the 1-pin stayed disgustingly still. A converted spare and a strike later, he had a 279 game and not a 300.

"I was in over my head," he said. "All the other players had gathered around and that's a normal thing. But I wish they wouldn't have. So many games like that get ruined because all of a sudden everybody comes over to watch and nobody else is bowling. The concentration is all on you. Some guys can handle it. At the time, I was a young punk. I just couldn't handle it."

In other words, he choked. Collapsed like a soufflé in an earthquake. Folded like a card table.

On the other hand, maybe not. It's worth considering that he wasn't going to throw strikes every shot for the rest of his life, and that after 15 in a row the law of averages just caught up.

It's conceivable that he just missed, and that if a spare in a 279 game had come in the second frame instead of the 10th, it would have been high spirits, back-slapping and cold ones all around. What isn't conceivable is that anyone at the alley was more disappointed than he was.

"I like to compete," he said. "I like winning. It's more fun. Yeah, I was pretty mad about it at the time."

The question of whether he choked – or threw the game of a lifetime – all depends on who is making the call, their point of view and to what extent they're "telling it like it is."

It's not like he meant to miss that head pin.

Shaking off his foiled bid at the 300 wasn't that difficult for the guy whose name would become synonymous with WJOL radio in Joliet because carrying on and making the best of things is what you learned to do growing up in the Depression Era. You were happy to even have a bowling bag to put your primeval cork ball inside of, let alone that you had the 25 cents to play a couple of games. You were glad to have much of anything back then, because food in the refrigerator and a house with working heat and plumbing weren't always a given. You can more easily feel like the luckiest guy in the world when you already know what really-unlucky feels like.

"I am so glad I grew up in the era I did," Don said. "It was just a different world, a different life. People were different back then."

During the first half of 20th century America you said things like "swell" and "hep-cat" and wore goofy-looking fedoras. You also kept your keys in the car ignition so you wouldn't lose them, and you didn't lock your house doors because the only thing that could have come of that was accidentally locking yourself out.

"It was fun growing up in those days because everything was enjoyable," Don said. "We played baseball from dawn to dusk in a lot over by Bluff Street, and we manicured the field ourselves. Not everybody had gloves, so we shared. Nobody had a lot of money back then, so we'd sew up the baseball when the cover came off and nail the bats together when they broke. You could break off some nice curves with a taped-up ball, believe me. It was a better life because there was no trouble out there. Everybody got along."

Don is a golden-ager discouraged as the next guy about the national decline of civility, but whatever shreds of antipathy he harbors toward the changing world are directed at behavior and not at individuals. He's annoyed that ballplayers need a contract year to get motivated; he loathes football's choreographed end-zone celebrations of the self; and he's disgusted that not only can many major leaguers not bunt a baseball, but that they don't seem too worried about it, either.

Don Ladas isn't from the old school. He's from the school they tore down to build the old school.

Despite the economic valleys that defined the stony quality of life in the 1930s – or maybe because of them – Don says there was a greater sense of community. Priorities were much different. You didn't tempt ridicule by wearing an off-the-rack suit, or a T-shirt without a designer logo. A fashion faux-pas back then was a misspelled word on your sandwich board.

But Don recalls that what America lacked in prosperity was mitigated by a prevailing sense of decency and propriety. Fair play and mutual respect were standard operating procedures his generation grew up with. The ego wasn't fed and watered as it would be in the I'm-OK-You're-OK years to follow. Self-promotion in that era was roundly mocked, and loophole-seeking businessmen who violated the spirit of a handshake deal were scorned.

It will be hard for future generations to appreciate the challenges that life in the early 21st centuries presented, such as the need to use your own fingertips to press all those numbers on the keypad of your cell phone/camera/recorder. In the same vein, it is impossible today to grasp the nature of what life was like in the Depression Era.

"You didn't worry about someone shooting you back then, for one thing," Don said. "People came out of those times appreciating what they had a lot more than today because they really had to work for it. You appreciate what you have when you've earned it. I think in a lot of cases that's missing today."

Every bit the sports fanatic now as he was 70 years ago, Don feels that another thing missing today is appreciation of the team effort, the implicit personal sacrifice as a means toward the end of winning as a group.

"I've seen baseball players today with their team down by a couple of runs late in a game, swinging at the first pitch," Don says. "That's something that was just never done. You need base runners in that situation. Now it's all about beefing up your statistics to get that big money on your next contract. Baseball used to be a real team game."

And in any sport, when you made a nice play you didn't feel moved to announce it to the world. Football players today premeditate their get-a-load-of-me end zone schtick; often they don't even need six points for a reason to break into an interpretive ode to the id.

"You see guys now making a sack or a tackle for loss, and they'll get up and run 10, 15 yards away from the pile to go pose, or flex their muscles," Don said. "And their team might be down by two touchdowns and they're doing that nonsense. That's why I loved Barry Sanders when he played. He let his game do the talking. He'd score and give the ball to the ref and that was it. Not that a guy can't stick his head up high if he's a good player, but some of the cockiness is for the birds. Sometimes I have to turn the TV off when I see it.

"It's not just in sports today, but in general. It's a different world now, all the way around. You don't like to see it happen. I don't want my kids to grow up that way, and I'm sure other parents don't like seeing their kids grow up like that. You've got to have confidence in life, but some of this stuff, standing at home plate to admire your home run instead of running right away, it doesn't make sense. I don't know. It's just … ."

But Don drifts off, stopping himself before delving into a full-scale assault on the swollen ego of the .260-hitting multi-millionaire. Equal parts pragmatist, humanist and logical positivist, Don is forever looking on the bright side. He sees vertically challenged, gravity-enhanced, chronologically gifted and folically impaired where others see short, fat, old and bald.

His working philosophy has always been to live and let live, and if you don't like the way he does things then you're cordially invited to take a hike. But no hard feelings. He might even note that you're doing a whale of a job with that hike.

Ultimately, he concedes that mourning the passing of an innocent era is useless, and that spewing bile is a drag on your well-being. So he goes silent. When you're the nicest guy in the world and you can't say something good about someone, the default mode is dead air.

Born at St. Joseph's Hospital in Joliet on December 23, 1928 to Gus and Catherine (Leona) Ladas, Don arrived on time, and the die was cast.

It was once suggested that eighty percent of success in life is showing up, and to that end he has batted 1.000. He never missed a day at Joliet Township High School, Joliet Junior College or Bradley University.

Gus Ladas, a Greek immigrant who came to America when he was 13 years old, instilled the work ethic into his sons – Don came almost two years after his brother Chuck – that proved to be durable. Wracked by excruciating back pain, respiratory difficulty and an array of other ailments in his late 70s, Don kept alive an uncanny 40-year streak of never having missed a day of work.

Eager to tap into the opportunity that life in the United States offered, Gus Ladas opened a restaurant on Bluff and Jefferson Streets in Joliet when Don was in fourth grade. Gus was convinced that there were no obstacles that hard work couldn't surmount, and he gave Chuck and Don their first job, tending the simmering drums of confection that would be made into the candy that was sold in the sweets section of the restaurant.

"I was in the back room, stirring the big vats of chocolate," Don said. "My favorite was the chocolate peanut clusters, but we had every kind of candy there. On Easter and Valentine's Day we'd make the chocolate eggs and hearts. It was great. We had all that access to candy any time we wanted."

Gus used reverse psychology to deal with the very literal dilemma of having kids in a candy store. He gave his sons the green light one day that was as bewildering as it was wonderful: Damn the dentist chair! Full speed ahead! The face-stuff was on.

"He said we should go ahead and eat whatever we wanted because he thought we might get sick enough to where we wouldn't abuse the access we had to the candy," Don said. "And it worked. I got sick, really sick. After that day, I never overdid it on the peanut clusters, or anything else we sold."

To the relief of his digestive tract, his next job was less sugar-intensive. On the weekends he worked the corner of Bluff and Jefferson, selling the Chicago Herald Examiner – which would later become the Sun Times – and the Chicago Tribune. He'd wile away the moments between sales pondering the big world around him, a happy kid compelled by the notion that there were no strangers out there but rather a bunch of friends who he hadn't met yet.

"Every Saturday I sold newspapers on that corner," Don said. "It was the busiest corner in Joliet at the time. There was a supermarket on one side of the street – Lincoln Bakery and Grocery – and Adler's on the other side, where they serviced all the boats that came through on the river. Both places did a lot of business, so it was a busy atmosphere, a busy street. One time a guy got hit by a car right on the corner where I was standing. Everybody was kind of shocked and just stood there, but my dad ran out in traffic and dragged the guy off to the side. The guy had a broken leg, I guess. My dad might've saved the guy's life because if he'd been hit again, he'd have been dead. There was a lot of traffic because there were only two lanes back then.

"But because it was busy, it was good for business. That was my spot. I had the good territory. I got a penny for every paper I sold."

A cashed-up youngster back in the '30s could go to a movie in downtown Joliet, plop down his dime and make a day of it.

"On Sundays there were about eight or 10 of us who went to the old Princess Theater on Jefferson and Chicago Streets," said Don, who has outlived all of those childhood cohorts. "It was a nickel for popcorn and a nickel for a candy bar. Gum was a penny a stick, or if you wanted a whole pack that was a nickel, too. Yeah, if I made a dollar on a Sunday morning, I could go wild at the theater that afternoon and still have change."

There wasn't a great deal of variety at the Princess Theater, but that was fine with Don and his St. John's grade school chums. They were riveted to the big screen anyway, lost in the latest tale of America's favorite half-naked swinger.

"Buster Crabbe played Tarzan when we first saw it there," Don said. "He was an athlete before he became an actor. He won a gold medal in swimming in the 1932 Olympics. They also had 15 episodes of the Lone Ranger at the Princess Theater. They showed one episode every week, so that way they got you coming back ... you know, Johnny Weissmuller also played Tarzan. He won *five* gold medals at the Olympics."

Don was only peripherally aware of radio in the 1930s, and as yet oblivious to how it would become the fount of his professional existence. As a young kid his dreams were still running along the lines of World Series two-out grand slams.

But radio's influence was spreading rapidly throughout the land. It is a matter of record how the country heaved a collective sigh of relief after learning that the "War Of The Worlds" was merely a made-for-radio drama and not a live broadcast of an outer space invasion.

H.G. Wells's seminal alien spoof aired in 1938, six years after President Franklin Roosevelt had given his first radio "fireside chat" urging Americans to hang in there because the economic straits they were enduring were temporary.

That was true, but only in the sense that a decade itself is temporary. The unemployment rate never fell below 14 percent throughout the 1930s. For an understanding of how far up the social strata the hard times had reached, consider the likes of those who turned up at the Zero Ice House.

Don didn't have the vaguest notion of what an appearance fee was back when he was seven years old. All he knew was that when he and Chuck and his dad went to the Zero Ice House on nearby Summit Street, he was going to see some really important baseball players.

Professional ballplayers in that era were ecstatic to be getting paid for playing a game they loved, the only drawback being that they didn't get paid much. All of them worked regular jobs in the offseason. Those with high name-recognition, including cultural icons like Babe Ruth and Lou Gehrig, could supplement their income making appearances at various business venues.

Ruth was the highest-paid professional athlete of his time, signing a contract with the New York Yankees for an eye-popping $70,000 back in the late '20s. If anyone was immune to the ravages of the depression, it seemed, it was Babe Ruth.

But in addition to being the biggest star of his era, and baseball's undisputed champion reaper of legal tender, the Babe was also an accomplished bon vivant. Gargantuan home runs by day were matched by heroic intakes of alcohol at night. Like Gehrig, and most every other American in the '30s, Ruth was strapped for dough.

Although the Zero Ice House was one of the service industries vital to the public in the days before the refrigerator/freezer became a household item, it was nonetheless an unlikely forum for two of the game's greatest players of all time. In any event, the afternoon there with Dad and Chuck was Don's first of what would be many brushes with famous athletes.

"Today they'd probably get hundreds of thousands of dollars for showing up there," Don says. "I don't know what they got back then, probably 25 bucks."

It is left to guess what a Hall of Famer like Gehrig might say in an ice house – "Today, I consider myself the coldest man on the face of this earth" – or whether the Bambino was actually hailing a cab on Summit Street and not pointing to the exact spot where the foreman would stack the next block of ice. Even the strongest memories forged onto the mind of a seven-year-old are hazy.

"I don't remember a word of what they talked about," Don says. "I was too young. They just gave some sort of spiel. I just remember they were two really famous ball players up there, right in Joliet. I remember I enjoyed being there with them. Guys like Luke Appling and Ted Lyons came down there, too."

Don then points out that Lyons, a White Sox pitcher, was often used as a pinch-hitter, that as his career wound down he pitched only on Sunday afternoons, that he once threw a no-hitter that took only 67 minutes and that during one season he had 20 starts and 20 complete games. Don does that a lot, reciting factoids and tangential stories relevant to a conversation. The nicest guy in the world is an ambulant, articulate reference book.

Don's emotional investment in baseball was evident on the night of April 16, 1941, after Cleveland's Bob Feller had thrown an opening-day no-hitter at the Chicago White Sox.

"I cried that night," he said. "I really did. I was upset. I took all of the Sox's losses to heart."

Don is endlessly compassionate. He is diplomatic down to his shoes. But there has never been a question to which side of the Second City his baseball loyalties lay.

"He's not a Republican or Democrat," his daughter Sheri said. "He'll vote for the best candidate in an election. The only thing he's ever declared is that he's a Sox fan."

If Don cried a little when Feller threw his no-no, he also died a little each of the five times the Cubs won pennants before his 17th birthday, while his White Sox were winning squadoosh. His frustration may have eased as the Cubbies lost all five of those World Series, but if he did any serious gloating about those Cubs defeats, he waited until he got home.

Death in the family, divorce and relocating households are considered the top three sources of stress an immune system can endure. A championship-game loss by your favorite team can also be a downer worthy of the Top 10. So there was no sense kicking someone when they were really down, Cubs fan or not.

Good-natured bragging rights were another story. When WGN-TV telecast its first baseball game, on April 16, 1948, it was a Cubs-Sox exhibition game won by the White Sox 4-1. The usual mild teasing was dished out to Cubs supporters in the neighborhood, but because it was only an exhibition game it was Trash Talk Lite. Serious fans on both sides know the difference between a meaningful game and a show-pony run-through.

Rubbing it in face-to-face when the Sox or Cubs lose a World Series, on the other hand, is hitting where it hurts. It isn't the done thing.

In fact, there may come a time when fans on both sides of the Cubs-Sox chasm come to grips with the fact that the antagonism is only a mix of their own personal envy and unfulfilled expectations, a microcosm of everything that's gone wrong in life. Some of Don's best friends are Cubs fans. He wouldn't wish ill on any of them, or undertake to strike a nerve in their sports-loving psyche. Eventually, the usefulness of the whole Chicago baseball feud comes into question.

A Sox fan in a one-up debate with a Cubs fan at the start of the 2008 season could – if he were that kind of guy – rekindle memories of the North Siders' gold-standard collapse of 1969, or talk about how their fans can't keep their hands in their pockets long enough to let them close out their first pennant in 58 years, or that in the teams' most recent postseason appearances the White Sox were 11-1 and won it all, while the

Cubs got swept by a team that went on to get swept by a team that went on to get swept.

But that would be pointless.

Gus Ladas and his brother opened Joliet's first bowling alley in a building by the Rialto Theater that is now the Hub restaurant. Don was in sixth grade, and in love.

"I thought bowling was the greatest game in the world," he said. "It was in my blood, I guess you could say. I loved everything about it."

Ladas Brothers Bowling Alley would be Don's home away from home throughout much of his adolescence because that's where the action was. And at the heart of that action was the scorer's table. Don's engine idles high, and runs best in heavy traffic.

"I was the kind of guy who liked to keep score," he said. "That way you stayed on top of the action. You were in the middle of everything, of everyone. With the automatic scorekeeping today, an awful lot of bowlers don't know how to keep score."

Don liked being the one telling you that you could still finish with a 196, or when a strike would mathematically seal a win for your team.

"I just like being around the action," he said. "I like being around people. I've always liked being around people."

In the first game he ever bowled, Don slung his cork globule to the tune of an 81, with one spare and no strikes. This was done in street shoes, before bowling alley proprietors noticed that street shoe scuff marks only served to ugly up the place, and started insisting customers wear bowling shoes or play in their stocking feet.

"Chuck liked to bowl, too, although not as much as I did," Don said. "He was a natural. He was good at everything he did – swimming, baseball, bowling. Although really he was probably best at fighting. He was 5-10 but he'd take on guys a lot bigger than him. He'd win those fights, too. And he always stuck up for me. If someone looked at me wrong, he'd pop 'em in the mouth."

The brothers were best friends and had similar interests, if disparate characteristics. Don had warning-track power and sprayed the ball to all fields. Chuck was a pull hitter who could knock one out. Chuck was taller, sinewy, quick-tempered and smoked like a tire fire. Don was short, slight, hated the smell of smoke and only occasionally dabbled in the pugilistic rituals of hormone-fueled boys feeling out their place in the alpha chain.

"We had a lot of good times, Chuck and I," Don said. "He treated me well, and so did his friends. Except that I was the only guy in the group who didn't smoke, and sometimes they'd all blow smoke at me to tease me. Chuck was a nice guy. But if he had a few drinks, it seemed like it wound him up. He didn't care how old or how big a guy was. If someone irritated him, he was going to battle him."

The longest fight Don ever saw was between his brother and a barber. It wasn't a bad haircut that set off the brawl; the barber had stepped in to try and break up a fight between Chuck and someone else.

"Chuck took him wrong," Don said. "The guy wasn't going after him. But they fought and they were really going at it, all over the street, up a hill. The barber finally went down, though. It was a long fight.

"I don't think I ever saw him lose a fight, either. He could really handle his dukes. If he was around today doing that, I'm afraid someone would shoot him. It was an interesting life growing up with him. When he went into the Navy, I thought, well, if I was going to get beaten up, I was going to get beaten up."

There were new friends and opponents for Don and Chuck to make when the Ladases moved to a house on Seeser Street on Joliet's west side, where Don finished his junior high school days at St. Patrick's.

To maintain the flow of walking-around money, he worked as a pin setter, earning a modest five cents a game. A pin setter's job required standing in the pits at the end of the lanes and loading the fallen pins into a receptacle that guided them back into place on the lane by a set of levers and hooks.

"There was a little knob underneath at the end of the lane, and you'd put your foot there, push it down, and you were set to bowl again," Don said.

A nickel per game was a bit light even by 1940s standards, but nothing that a little initiative couldn't overcome. Don soon figured out how to "jump pits," or work two lanes at once, and double his income. If things got boring back there – and they did – one of his co-workers was there to break the monotony.

"There was a guy I worked with who played football for Joliet Township named 'Goo' Martin, and he could cross his eyes so all you could see were the whites of them," Don said. "He'd sneak up on you with those eyes and act like a spooky guy."

Goo's faces were definitely scarier than any of the balls thrown by a group of women's senior league bowlers one afternoon. Their shots inched down the lane at earthworm speed, and after a few frames Don could see that earning this nickel was going to take a while. So rather than stand back and let the ball drop into the pit, as was the practice, he would catch the balls as they dropped off the lane to move things along, defiant of any possible harm from flying pins.

"They didn't appreciate that, I don't think," Don said. "They seemed kind of upset I was doing it. But they were bowling so slow."

Senior women's leagues notwithstanding, flying pins were always a potential danger to pin setters. Don once took an airborne 7-pin off the noggin from a shot by a player whose reaction to it was a little too Marquis de Sade for Don's tastes. As he winced in pain and rubbed the welt, the bowler laughed.

Don was furious, not because he got hurt but because of the disregard for his feelings shown by the hyena at the other end of the lane. That's not how it worked in the old school. If someone was hurt, you asked if they were OK, especially if the injury was of your doing. If you were disinclined to even feign concern, then you at least waited until get home to laugh about it.

As the twenty-something bowler mirthfully howled over the head-knock, an enraged Don crawled out of the pit and threw a bowling pin at him. It missed, whizzing past the ear of the startled malefactor by a few feet.

"I don't think he meant to do it," Don said. "Obviously, how could you try to do that? That stuff happens when you're standing back there and the pins are flying. You get hit sometimes, and that time I got hit in the head. Pretty hard, too.

But the guy was laughing his butt off. You don't like someone laughing at you when you're hurt. I'm just glad I didn't hit him with the pin. That wasn't smart."

It was not smart – understandable, perhaps – but it was a fitting demonstration of how human mammals are capable of the full 360 degrees of behavior. Just as a cat burglar may help an old lady cross a street, so too can the nicest guy in the world lose it one day and whip a bowling pin at a jerk.

For the most part, Don never ran afoul of the law as a youngster – unless you count the time he deceived the federal government. Too young for tax evasion or inside trading, his transgression was of a more quaint nature, almost honorable given the temperament of the United States at the time.

Prior to Japan's bombing of Pearl Harbor, 83 percent of the people in the country were against idea of America's joining the war that had been raging in Europe for more than two years.

After the attack on the naval base in Hawaii that killed 2,350 people, however, approximately one million Americans enlisted. Chuck was spoiling for a fight again, only this time his fury was directed at something other than a local greaser who stole his cigarettes.

"He wanted to go fight in the war," Don said. "He was mad that we got attacked. He got mad a lot, but he was really upset that we were attacked. So he wanted to join the military and go fight. But he was too young. He was only 16."

So Chuck entreated Don to forge their father's name on Chuck's enlistment papers. As is often the case when the older sibling exerts his will, the younger brother went along with it.

The Voice Of Joliet

The timing was right for the caper because Mom and Dad were away on vacation. Chuck got as far as the physical exam before his true age was discovered, and he was sent back to Joliet. Having sorted out with the authorities the innocuous nature of the violation, and their having determined that it was more virtuous than criminal, the matter was dropped. No harm, no foul, no police record.

"That was stupid," Don said. "I don't know what I was thinking."

In high school he wasn't thinking much about his studies. Don says he mailed it in throughout those four years at Joliet Township, pulling mostly C's on his report card before getting serious in college, where he got A's and B's. In high school he was thinking about playing baseball for JT, and how much fun it was going to be wearing the Steelmen uniform. Don fairly salivated at the idea of facing pitchers from other schools, playing with brand-new white baseballs on a field with chalk baselines and real umpires calling balls and strikes. Maybe there would even be a crowd watching. He'd thought about that a lot. It's the kind of thing you fantasize about when you're 10 or 11 years old playing pitcher's-hands-out in the sandlot.

Don had the tools, too: good hands, quick bat, nice speed out of the box and a good head for the game.

"I might not have had long ball power, but I could get the job done," he said.

Those who saw him playing in his 50s and 60s, still ripping line drives and snaring hard grounders at the softball benefit games, would not argue.

But a funny thing happened to him on his way to a satisfying high school baseball career. Funny when you got home, anyway.

There are several ways for young ballplayers to ensure getting cut at their high school tryouts, the most popular of which is to have no talent. Another way, lesser-known but equally effective, is to throw a baseball off your coach's head.

It was the latter that kept Don from making the team at JT.

During some pre-practice loosening up, he let fly a toss whose trajectory ended fatefully at a space where the coach had wandered.

Seconds earlier the coach was the man in full form, grandly pacing the terrain, surveying with a critical eye the group he would be marshaling to glory. With the unmistakable *pong* of hardball meeting skull, however, the would-be Connie Mack had been reduced to Curly Howard.

Less than thrilled with his starring role in this unintended gag reel, the coach unloaded on his player, and Don's high school baseball days were effectively cashiered.

"He was all worked up about it," Don recalls. "I felt bad about it, too. I didn't mean to hit the guy. He shouldn't have been where he was! It was just one of those things."

If only the coach hadn't changed directions like he did just before Don threw. If only Don had gotten a better grip on the seams. If only the guy on the other end of the catch had quicker reactions. If, if, if.

But the coach wasn't hurt badly, so if you're keen on silver linings, there you are. No harm, no foul.

Sort of. No baseball, either.

The coach was Aubry "Fizz" Wills, who went on to establish himself as one of Joliet's football and baseball coaching icons – his 678 baseball victories with Joliet Junior College was a mark that stood at the school for four decades until it was broken by Wayne King.

Don and Fizz got past that incident and became friendly a few years later when Don was covering Wills's Joliet JC baseball games for the Joliet Herald News.

"He was a real character," Don said. "A lot of people didn't like him because he did things a different way, but I thought he was a great guy."

Fizz certainly had the capacity for laughs, at least during those moments he wasn't taking a Rawlings off the temple. Bob Gutierrez, who played left field for JJC, remembers the Great Ham Sandwich Incident that Wills was responsible for creating.

Because he had wheels and because he was happy to do it, Don drove half of the Joliet JC baseball team to many of the road games he covered. Coach Wills drove the other half.

"We played a game against the Great Lakes Naval Academy," said Gutierrez, who coached high school tennis in Joliet for 30 years. "And I can't remember if we won the game, but they invited us for a ham dinner afterward. They treated us very nicely. We asked if we could take some leftover ham sandwiches back home with us, and they said sure, so we put them in the trunk of Don's car.

"We got to the gate, and one of the guards asked us to get out of the car and open the trunk. Of course, we thought we were in some sort of trouble. But we weren't smuggling anything. We didn't know what was going on. The guard said he heard that we'd stolen some ham from the kitchen. We figured we'd be in trouble if they didn't believe us, but we finally convinced them that the people in the kitchen had made it for us and given the sandwiches to us. As it turned out, it was Coach Wills who told the guard that we stole the ham. He was messing around and playing a joke on us."

"I was a little bit worried for a while there," Don said. "But that was Fizz Wills for you. You had to know that guy. He was a tremendous coach."

Covering a Joliet JC game once for WJOL, Don brought one of the station's new engineers along for the night, which culminated with a stop at Galli's bar – where the owner, Art "Boots" Galli, was a friend of Don's.

"Joliet lost that night, one of the few games they lost that year," Don said, "but we all went over to Galli's. Fizz was there with his wife, who never said a word. She just drank. We had a table, and we stayed pretty late. The new engineer was drunk to the gills. Everybody was having a good time, in fact. I remember dropping the engineer off at his house, and he was slurring so badly you could hardly understand him. As we pulled up to his place he asked me, 'Wh … wha … whaddy you guys do when you win?'"

With baseball off the table and bowling decades away from being a high school team sport, Don lettered in wrestling at Joliet Township. He competed in the 95-pound division, winning more often than not, but not as often as teammates Earl D'Amico, Dave Shapiro and John Govoni. All three were state champions.

Don had known Govoni for years. They both worked on Gus Ladas's farm about eight miles west of Joliet, cutting asparagus. Don knows it was about eight miles away because he walked home once, angry at his dad for making them cut the asparagus a second time after a heavy rain.

"It was so muddy through some of those fields and farms I had to cross, it was like quicksand," Don said. "I wasn't sure I was going to make it home that day.

"But Don Govoni and I had fun working there. He might've been the best wrestler I've ever seen. He was like a monkey, a really amazing natural athlete. Once he learned all the moves and holds, he was an unbeatable wrestler."

D'Amico, a successful Joliet businessman whose path would cross with Don's often throughout their professional lives, went undefeated in his junior year en route to winning the title in the 133-pound division. Also a star wrestler at Purdue, D'Amico summarized the feelings of the whole Steelmen squad toward their pint-sized teammate.

"I don't know anybody who doesn't like Don Ladas," he said.

"Earl was as tough as they come," Don said. "And Govoni won at 138 pounds, but he could've won at any weight class. He went on to Arkansas State and went into the Hall of Fame there."

And Don tore off on another dazzling recital of obscure factoids.

Wrestling was fun. Bowling was more fun. You could eat during bowling season, for one thing, and nobody at the alley was trying to twist your arm off.

Through constant practice Don's average crept up into the 170s during the time he set pins at the Elks bowling alley. When the lanes were dead, he would get his solo game going, rolling the cork ball, running to the other end, setting his own pins, running back and repeating the process over and over.

He organized mini-tournaments at school, pitting himself and his classmates against some of the Joliet Township coaches and teachers.

"And the kids won!" Don said. "Some of those coaches were good bowlers, too, better than me. It's a good thing we beat them in bowling, because there's no way we could've beaten them at anything else. The guy who organized the coaches' team was Don Kinlan. I've never seen a guy do more pushups with one arm. He was just a great, healthy guy. He was a wrestling coach and at practice he'd always say, 'Drive, LAY-dus, drive!' He called me LAY-dus."

Don, whose last name is pronounced LADD-us, pushed his average up to 185 by his senior year in his high school career. In his four-night-a-week adult bowling life he reached a high-water mark of 189.

"I never thought about trying to turn pro, not me," he said. "If you don't have a 200 average, forget it. The requisite now is 190, but you won't find too many bowlers with a 190 average trying out for the Tour. There are too many guys way over 200. Some of these guys bowl 70, 80 games a week. You look at a bowling tournament and think, 'They're only bowling three games.' But you don't see what they go through to qualify."

Besides, if he went pro, he wouldn't get to keep score.

Baseball players used to leave their gloves out in the field when the half-inning was over. Basketball used to have a jump ball after every basket. But of all the evolutionary changes in sports, Don says the biggest ones have come in bowling.

"Back in the '50s and '60s, most players didn't use a separate ball to pick up spares," he said. "A lot of guys now go into a bowling house with half a dozen balls. You see guys' wives carrying a couple of balls for them as they walk in there. Lane conditions mean so much now, and I really admire today's bowlers' ability to read the lanes and adjust to them. They throw two or three different balls in a game and they know exactly which one they're going to use on any different lane. I think it's uncanny. That's why in the past, if we had one 700 series per month, it was really something. Now we get some every night. *Every night.*"

Don played with and against Jim Stefanich, a Lockport, Illinois, resident who played on the Professional Bowling Association Tour and on the U.S. Pro Golf Tour.

Stefanich, who won 14 Professional Bowling Association tournaments and was named Sporting News Player of the Year in 1967, is best remembered for bowling a perfect game at the '74 Midas Open. He was the third player to roll a 300 on live national TV.

"He got out of bowling because of all the technological changes," Don said. "He thought all the advances with the ball and lane conditions and everything else were taking the challenge out of the game.

"A guy like Stefanich, there's someone who could handle the pressure. I can't tell you how he did it, but he was like no one else around. Some guys would get mad at Jim for not saying hello when he was playing in a pro tournament. But he was strictly concentration. When you're as good as he was, you figure that's what he had to do. That was his way of life.

"Put yourself in his shoes. He's bowling for money. That was his livelihood. Jimmy was a really different guy. He was 14 or 15 years old and he was beating all the adults. His dad used to put money in the pot for him – we'd all kick in some money and have a little side competition on league nights – and most guys would buy drinks when they won. But not Jim. He put the money in his pocket. We kidded the heck out of him. We just couldn't straighten him out."

For Don's part, he couldn't straighten out his roll. He threw a backup ball, meaning that as a right-hander his shots would break left-to-right instead of the usual right-to-left hook.

"I screwed up my hand because of it," he said. "Now I can't even put my middle finger in a ball. I have a little niche carved out where I lay my finger on top of it."

Don had his appendix removed after graduating from JT and then went on a huge growth spurt.

"I went from 95 pounds to 180 in about one year," he said. "I have no idea why that happened when it did, or if it was related to the surgery. I just know I've been at 180 ever since."

This wasn't a bacon double cheeseburger and large fries bump up to 180, either. Five-mile runs are a proven antidote to onset middle-aged lard.

"The more you lose yourself in something bigger than yourself, the more energy you will have."

Of all the many positive mottos and messages put forth by Norman Vincent Peale, the above may best reflect Don's commitment to the people of Joliet. His lot has always been about serving the community, giving the athletes their due and making sure everyone got a piece of the spotlight.

It's a grind, though, with the endless loop of banquets, benefits and big games to attend. Even a guy in great shape needs a little extra in reserve to meet the demands of a non-stop schedule.

Running gave Don the extra bit in the tank. His love for bowling is well-known in Joliet, as is his passion for racquetball and his ability to hit a softball to all fields. But not everyone is aware what a serious runner he has been all his adult life.

It can be estimated how fast and how much running is required to lose weight. A general rule of thumb is that a deficit of 3500 calories is needed to drop one pound, for example.

But there is no charting the emotional benefits from the regular "oxygen flush" that a run provides, or how running tightens the mind-body connection vital to an aligned, self-realized existence.

"I'm lucky to have been healthy all my life," Don said. "I know that running had a lot to do with it. I'd run five miles a day, five times a week for as long as I can remember."

In the early 1980s Don was on an assignment at a field near Northwestern University and asked a football coach if he had a minute to talk about one of his players.

"I'm kind of pressed for time," the coach said. "I have to go for a run and then catch a plane right after that. Sorry. Unless … are you a runner?"

Don had already put in his five-miler by the time the coach asked, but in the quest for the interview and the better story – the striving for excellence – he had no problem going the extra mile, as it were.

The coach was George Allen, the former Bears defensive coordinator who had also been head coach of the Los Angeles Rams and Washington Redskins.

"He was great," Don said. "We didn't get into a whole lot of depth, but he was very forthcoming and interesting. After about a mile, I forgot I was running. That was the first time – the only time – that I ever went for a run holding a recorder and a notebook."

The 1950s may have been the most consequential decade of Don's life because during that time he went three-for-three in critical, path-defining decisions.

The first decision came after a conversation with a veteran colleague at the railroad where Don worked for a couple of years after dropping out of college.

Working on the railroad, he inspected couplings and air brake hoses, repaired and installed track and helped couple and uncouple train cars. Don would ride the handcar to areas where tracks needed repair, remove the handcar, do the repair work, put the handcar back on the track, ride it back, punch out and go home.

"I worked the jackhammer a lot, too," he said. "And I was a flagger. A flagger would signal when a train was coming so that the workers could get off the track until the train passed."

It was honest, productive work, and because it paid well it was an attractive gig for a young man of the Depression Era.

But it was also repetitive and tedious, and the long-term prospects were limiting to an adventurous soul in the prime of life. Those he worked alongside were decent enough, even if they seemed to have accepted a fate that Don was not ready to.

"I remember working with this one guy, every day he's whistling and all this," Don said. "We got to talking and I asked him how long he'd been doing this. He said he'd been there 29 years. I said, 'Holy cripes, 29 years! What are you going to do when you leave here?' He'd dropped out of school, just like I had.

"He said, 'Leave here? I'm not gonna leave here. There's nothing else I can do.' Right then I thought, yeah, it's good money, but 29 years? I don't want to work here 29 more days."

Having caught a glimpse of the Ghost of Don Ladas Future – tired, sore, replacing railroad ties, glancing at his watch every 10 minutes and whistling for fear of going crazy – Don decided that the prospect of becoming a railroad lifer was too much. So, as it is phrased in construction-work jargon, he "dragged up." He quit the job and enrolled at Joliet Junior College.

"It was a decision I was glad I made," he said. "Don't get me wrong, it wasn't the worst job in the world. But it just wasn't what I wanted to do all my life."

At JJC he studied journalism and took the part-time job writing for the Joliet Herald News. He went from junior college to Bradley University, where he graduated with a degree in journalism in 1954.

Don's relationship with the written word gave him a good foundation for a career in sports journalism, and also brought an unexpected dividend.

With baseball in his blood like it was for virtually every American boy in the 1930s and '40s, Don held the Boston Red Sox's Ted Williams in high esteem.

From New York to St. Louis, in fact, American baseball fans of every leaning could not help but look up to the guy known as "Teddy Ballgame." Williams was the best pure hitter in the game, and arguably the best pure hitter ever – he is the last player to bat .400 over a season. He was also a World War II and Korean War hero.

Williams' career baseball statistics are remarkable not only in that they are some of the gaudiest offensive numbers posted in the modern era, but also in that they were compiled despite having lost almost five prime playing years to the service. Williams was a Marine fighter pilot who flew 38 missions in the two wars.

He rejoined the Red Sox after World War II but was called back to active duty in 1952 and missed most of that season, as well as most of the next season; he played in just six games in 1952 and 37 games in '53. Earlier that year he won the Air Medal for safely landing a plane whose hydraulic and electric systems were knocked out over North Korea.

In the summer of '53 he was selected to the American League all-star team, an oddity for one who played so few games but not so odd given his circumstances and track record. It was one of 17 times he made the all-stars. Almost finished with his second tour of duty with the Marines, Williams made it to Crosley Field in Cincinnati on July 14 but did not play in the game.

Instead, he watched from the box seats. Seated next to him were Bill Veeck, the guy who would go on to become owner of the White Sox, and a 24-year-old Don Ladas.

"It was the thrill of a lifetime," Don said. "I couldn't believe I was watching the All-Star Game with Ted Williams."

Williams, whose .344 career batting average earned him the auxiliary nickname of "The Splendid Splinter," had a piece of advice for the kid from Joliet, and Don was all ears.

"He said to me, 'If you're going to sit with us, kid, you're going to have to lose that tie.' I laughed and said, 'Hey, I'll take off my tie, my shirt, my shoes ... hell, my pants, too, whatever!' I was just so happy to be there," Don said.

It was Don's persuasive-argument skills, a talent that would come into play as an advertising salesman at WJOL, which led to that unforgettable summertime memory.

Sport Magazine sponsored a national writing contest earlier that year inviting readers to submit an essay supporting a position whether a player on a last-place team should or should not be allowed to win the Most Valuable Player award.

The contest was ultimately a battle of the parsing of semantics. In a strictly literal sense, the criterion for considering MVP candidates had always been understood as "where would the team be without him?" Logically, a last-place team can do no worse than finish last, and thus no player could be argued to have been indispensable in his team's drive to the cellar.

The idea for the contest was inspired by the controversy following the announcement of the 1952 MVP awards. Outfielder Hank Sauer hit .270 with 37 homers and 121 RBIs for the fifth-place Cubs, beating out not only pitcher Robin Roberts, who went 28-7 for the Philadelphia Phillies, but also pitchers Joe Black, who was 15-4 for the National League champion Brooklyn Dodgers, and Hoyt Wilhelm, who had a 15-3 mark with the second-place New York Giants.

In the American League, controversy also stirred when Philadelphia Athletics pitcher Bobby Shantz went 24-7 and won the MVP award despite playing on a team just four games over .500. He nosed out three players on the World Series champion New York Yankees: pitcher Allie Reynolds (20-8), second-year outfielder Mickey Mantle (.311, 23 HR, 87 RBIs) and catcher Yogi Berra (.273, 30 HR, 98 RBIs).

"I don't remember exactly what I wrote," Don said. "But my position was that no matter what team a guy is on, it should be more of a player-of-the-year type of award than a most-valuable-to-the-team thing. Even if the guy played on a last-placed team, my point was that in every game they played, he was the one who gave his team the best chance in that game. When I got the letter from the editor telling me I'd won, I was sure it was someone playing a joke on me."

If it was a joke, it was well-executed. The letterhead looked legit, and he couldn't imagine who among his friends would be motivated, or capable enough, to pull off such a hoax.

But he wasn't about to get "punk'd," either. His journalistic instincts to verify moved him to phone the editor of Sport. As the editor confirmed that the letter had in fact come from him, a nearly hyperventilating Don learned that he would not only be watching the game with a couple of baseball legends, but that he would also be hitting the party circuit in the lead-up to the game.

"I got treated like one of the players," he said. "Our seats were really good, too – right behind the dugout. It was just an unbelievable thrill."

Tie-less but still wearing pants, Don soaked up every pitch of the midsummer classic, won by the National League 5-1. His favorite team was well-represented; White Sox pitcher Billy Pierce started and threw three scoreless innings, and Sox outfielder Minnie Minoso went 2-for-2 for the AL, which only had five hits for the game.

It was worth noting that the two MVPs from the previous season, who inspired the whole notion for the contest, were having mediocre seasons and didn't make the all-stars.

"The whole thing was so special, I'll never forget it," Don said. "I didn't see Ted Williams before or after that, except to watch him play. But Bill Veeck never forgot me. Every time that I'd go up to Comiskey Park to cover a Sox game, he'd greet me: 'Hey, Don, how you doing?' I always thought that was something, that he'd remember me like that. He was a good guy, a regular guy."

Decades later, a member of Don's second-favorite pro baseball team in Chicago reinforced the argument he'd successfully made in '53. The Cubs finished last in the National League East Division in the 1987 season but salvaged a morsel of consolation when outfielder Andre Dawson hit 49 homers and won the NL MVP.

Reminded of how it was another Cubs player who duplicated the feat that set in motion his date with Ted Williams, Don graciously set aside all Cubs acrimony and paid homage to Sauer and Dawson.

"Uh ...," he said, "yeah."

The second good move Don made in his young adult life came in 1954 when a colleague recommended him as someone to consider for a sports slot on Joliet's nascent radio station, WJOL. He enjoyed writing sports for the paper, but the chance to explore unchartered vocational ground excited him.

"I've had a lot of fun in the radio business," he said. "I can't imagine doing anything else. I just figured it was worth a shot. I remember during my first broadcast I felt like there were a thousand people in that room watching me and listening."

When it was jokingly suggested that he could have shopped that number of listeners around to prospective advertisers, Don noted that it would have been him doing the shopping. Multitasking was the order of the day at the station, and like the PGA Tour golfers who must produce if they're interested in putting food on the table, Don sold advertising space to keep the show afloat.

Sales were a different sort of animal for Don. Hawking newspapers on a street corner as a 10-year-old was one thing. Cold-calling to pry unspent dollars from wary business owners was another.

"I didn't know what I was doing there, either," he said. "But I figured that until I got myself acclimated to it, I'd go for the smaller accounts first. I was doing Ten Pin Topics, so it seemed logical to go our strengths. I stayed away from the banks and car dealerships for a while and went to the bowling alleys and bars instead. That was our advertising base. Once I started to feel a little more knowledgeable about how it all worked, then I went for the big meat."

Don went selling in between his spots on the air, a schedule that typically that took up the whole day. His first broadcast was at 8:05 a.m., followed by one at 12:35 p.m., then 4:55, 6:25 and 10:55.

"I didn't have to do the late one, but I came in a lot of nights just to get the practice, just to do what I wanted to accomplish," he said. "Some nights I'd play a softball game and then come back in to do the 10:55 sports. I got five bucks for every game that I covered and a buck for each sportscast. For the first four or five years, that's all I was getting."

But while the manifold duties that the radio biz entailed made it a time-consuming job, he never counted himself as anything but lucky. He worked through the kinks of learning a new craft, improving every day, and on a sultry summer afternoon in 1956 he knew he'd arrived.

Don called the play-by-play of the Pony League championship game held in Washington, Pennsylvania, where Ingalls Park, the Joliet entry in the tournament, had just brought a national championship to the proud, blue-collar town previously known to the rest of the U.S. for steelwork and a prison.

Spotted in downtown Joliet by a confused friend who'd listened to the broadcast less than an hour earlier, Don was asked about the implausible return time from Pennsylvania to Illinois. How did he get home so quickly?

He still laughs at the memory of the question, the answer of which had neither to do with jet packs nor a bending of the space-time continuum.

Don had never worked with ticker tape before that tournament, but it didn't take long to get the hang of it. The pitch-by-pitch results of the game would come over the wire into the Western Union office on Scott Street, from where, against a background of piped-in crowd noise, he would recreate the tape results into a "live" broadcast. The information provided on the tape was minimal, though, and a hefty dose of ad-libbing was required to make the broadcast colorful and believable.

"The tape would just read 'S1' for strike one, or 'B1' for ball one, so I had to make up all the details," he said. "After a little while, I'd be saying things like, 'High and outside, that's ball three.' It was tough for the first couple of innings. Then I got into it. That was when I realized I could do this job. It was a real confidence-builder. When I got out of there, I realized I could handle anything in sports broadcasting because ultimately it was all about how much you knew about the game."

Leading the way for Ingalls Park was a young Ed Spiezio, whose three home runs in the tournament earned him the most valuable player award. Spiezio went on to an eight-year major league career that included three World Series appearances as an infielder with the St. Louis Cardinals.

The Cards won two of those Series, in 1964 and '67, and the Spiezio family would later complete a unique daily double when Ed's son Scott also played on two World Series champions, the 2002 Anaheim Angels and the '06 Cardinals.

"A lot of the other guys on the Ingalls Park team remember more about that Pony League tournament than I do, only because I went on further and played in so many other games after that," Ed Spiezio said. "I remember that the pitching there was dominating, and the caliber of teams was dominating. I also remember that it was raining in that last game, and that we had a big lead and tried to do what we could to get the game in.

"And of course when they had the celebrations afterward, Don was there. Don has been there all the time. Talk about someone who really knows everything about athleticism in Joliet from every angle. It's amazing he can remember all the people who have come out of there, everything they've done. He's fabulous. He really is."

Ed's late uncle Tony Spiezio was an outstanding bowler who once won the Joliet tournament with a 799 series.

"He had an 800-something before that, too," Ed said. "I remember we used to talk about the depths of the mind and what everyone is capable of. My uncle was really into that stuff. He called me once after he'd done a show with Don where they were going pretty deep into the mental side of sports. Tony said what a great, great interview it was. Don and I have had a lot of great hours, a lot of interesting interviews. No question, he's the voice of Joliet. No one comes close to him. He keeps close track of what the various local athletes are doing with their careers, what they're doing, if they're having trouble. If you want to know anything, you just go to Don."

As his influence grew in Joliet, so did his reputation in town as the go-to guy. Don got involved with every benefit dinner, fundraiser and charity outing that asked. He spearheaded the Multiple Sclerosis Softball Benefit that ran for 25 years and has worked with the Wish Upon A Star foundation for the past 29 years, to name two.

"The charities come to me, there are so many of them," Don said. "They're all good causes, too, so you always want to help people out. I just could never say no."

The founder and executive director of the Joliet branch of the Wish Upon A Star foundation approached Don with a novel fundraising idea about 30 years ago.

"I remember calling him in '79 to ask about a softball game in January, to ask if he had a date open around that time," Don West said. "He asked me why I was calling him now. He thought I was talking about plans in January for a game in July. When I told him that, no, the idea was to play a benefit softball game in the dead of winter, he thought I was a little bit off my rocker. But he committed to doing the game."

The game was a huge success from both a financial and entertainment standpoint.

"It was supposed to be a one-shot deal," West said. "But we were sitting at the Ingalls Park Athletic Club afterward, and Don said he thought we were on to something, and that we should have it again next year. I disagreed at first. I thought it was just a little different fantasy kind of thing to help raise money for children, for the Ronald McDonald House. But finally he convinced me that we should keep it going."

Last January was the 29th year of the Softball in the Snow classic, which has brought out the likes of Joliet-area professional ballplayers like pitchers Mark Grant, Steve Parris and Chris Michalak, outfielder Les Norman and infielder Ron Coomer.

As usual, Don was at the fore in getting the word out.

"Even when it was 66 below zero wind chill, Don stuck it out," West said. "We've played in a foot of snow. I've gone up to the press box at the ballpark with Don, and he's had me on the air with him doing a few innings of the broadcast."

Don kept score as he did the broadcast, of course. That's the best way to stay in the middle of the action, especially when you're stuck to the chair like a hunk of frozen stalagmite.

"Donnie never swayed," West said. "He's probably one of the most caring persons I've ever met, in all aspects of life. He's brought in so many celebrities to his MS Benefit in the summertime. When he asked me to play in it, it was the biggest thing to happen to me – to be a part of it, raising money for a good cause and playing against some big names. I'm sure there was a long list of people who would've loved to play. I'm very fortunate to know Don and his wonderful wife Mary Lou, and Sheri, Angie and Donnie Jr."

West had first met Don in the 1970s, when West was a defensive end at Joliet West High School. Don was doing his Coaches Corner show, a weekly spinoff of his regular "Shooting The Breeze" program on WJOL. Coaches Corner brought coaches together to analyze the games played earlier that night, and pulled in a large audience.

"We would all hurry up and shower after the games," West said. "Then we'd stop and get a couple cases, drive to a dirt road by the interstate and listen to Don Ladas on Coaches Corner. You'd hear the beer bottles clanging – we used to joke about how the coaches were out having a good time and they didn't know we were out having a good time, too – and we were all hoping Don would say our names on the radio. To hear our names on the radio was a big deal.

"Everybody looked up to Don, this huge pillar. We were in awe. Every young guy – whether it was a baseball, football or basketball player – if they saw Don Ladas at the game they thought, 'Hey, the big guy is here.' That's how much an impact he had on young people's lives."

West was joined by Don recently in granting a wish to a terminally ill child. Don wore his Wish Upon A Star jacket to the presentation.

"I told him the jacket was for him, and that he didn't really have to wear it to the functions we do," West said. "He said he wanted to wear it there, that he wears it with pride."

The weekly Coaches Corner programs and softball games in the snow were still years away when Don started at WJOL. As the newly named program director in 1954, he faced the knotty predicament of having no programs to direct.

The void didn't last long, and you didn't need tea leaves to see that the repertoire of new shows would include bowling.

He developed Ten Pin Topics program shortly after hiring in.

"I figured why not do bowling. It's what I knew," he said.

Ten Pin Topics was a finger on the pulse of the area's top players and tournament winners. But the show was really dedicated to the average player, the man or woman at the alley whose 120 average was secondary to the fact that they were out there playing.

"I mention as many people as I can because everyone likes to hear their name," Don said. "If some guy threw a 140 but picked up a little 3-10 split in the game, I'd report that. The show is still on the air, so I guess I must've done something right."

"Whispering" Joe Wilson, the soporific bowling announcer whose nickname says everything there is to know about his style, was a guest when Don did his first Joliet Bowlers Association banquet in 1957. Because he was on television, Wilson was the game's best-known media representative of the day, and the banquet drew a nice crowd – even if some came just to see if he would be using his inside voice there, too.

"He just talked normal," Don said. "Even if he'd have whispered, he was talking into a microphone."

Forty-eight more JBA emcee honors followed for Don, who evidently also did something right there.

His dedication to the advancement of bowling in the area included the creation of the Will County Sportsman, a semi-monthly broadsheet newsletter he published with Bob Drazkowski beginning in the early 1960s.

"I think the Joliet Herald News' sports section does a great job," Don said. "But at that time, I didn't think they were doing enough with bowling. That's why we put it out."

Big victories highlighted the year 1959, arguably the single most consequential year of Don's life.

For starters, the White Sox were making a run at the American League pennant.

The Sox couldn't hit the ball too well but they could throw it and catch it. Pitchers Early Wynn, Bob Shaw and Billy Pierce led the way, with shortstop Luis Aparicio and second baseman Nelson Fox anchoring a defense that preserved a lot of 3-2 and 4-3 wins.

"Obviously, you have to look at the 2005 Sox as one of my favorite teams because they won the World Series," Don said, still glowing three years after the fact. "But my all-time favorite Sox team might have been that '59 squad. They came out of nowhere. Guys like Jim Landis and Sherm Lollar and the whole pitching staff, really, all had good years. They got big hits and Aparicio stole a lot of bases. Nobody expected them to win it that year and that's what made it so special."

To a spirited White Sox fan dying to know what a pennant race felt like, the summer of the Go-Go Sox was a thousand angels massaging his heart.

The first-place Sox led Baltimore by a game when Mary Lou Werner walked into the office.

Don had seen Mary Lou before. She and her three sisters – Nancy (Diaz), Kathy (Klemm) and Joanne (Fitzgerald) – would join their mother Mary and father John at St. Mary's Church, where Don also went. One look at Mary Lou's soft, feminine features still radiating in 2008 leaves little wonder what kind of effect she had on young men back in 1959, when she hired in at WJOL.

"Oh, she was good-looking, alright," Don said. "She and her sisters all were. The guys at church definitely noticed that. I never thought I'd end up with her, though."

Hitting his stride as a salesman and broadcaster at WJOL in the summer of '59, Don was also pushing 30 and performing very much like a guy in his physical prime – running his daily five miles at a good clip, maintaining his 185 average at the alleys and stinging the softball and quenching his thirst with equal facility.

Something was slightly askew in his world, though. The new girl at work had got under his skin.

"I was a record librarian," Mary Lou said. "There was a staff of just five girls, but we all had to learn to do all the jobs because the staff was so small. We'd type up the daily log, which included the schedule of everything the announcers had to do – which advertisers were sponsoring which segments, things like that. Everything the announcers were doing that day, we had to tell them which program to go to, and at what time."

There was an interesting foreshadowing in that process, with Mary Lou working behind the scenes to prepare and enable Don's enterprise. But it was early in the relationship. They were still getting to know each other.

"We shared a desk in the hall. Don was always very friendly, very interesting. He was always a lot of fun," she said.

Friendly is what you would expect from the nicest guy in the world, and interesting is a natural by-product when you've been a VIP guest at the All-Star Game. Fun is what happens when you look at every day as an opportunity, an adventure, an event and a gift. Getting people to like you is just the other side of you liking them. Don liked people, and won them over with a natural ease.

But for all the accounts he wrapped up with his effective soft-sell approach, he never made a bigger close than the one he did over the next two years.

Don shifted his charm into overdrive, and Mary Lou was receptive. It might have been the easy way that he carried himself when the WJOL group got together at social functions, or the competitiveness he demonstrated in the softball games she watched him play. But what could also have ultimately won over the cute girl from Joliet was Don's ability to incite a smile.

"He made me laugh," Mary Lou said. "It wasn't a long courtship. The picnics we had with the group at WJOL, the baseball games, the Christmas parties. Frank O'Leary would be telling jokes all day. It was just a fun thing working there. It was a very low-key atmosphere at the station back then. Businesses aren't run like that today."

"There was more of a togetherness back then at WJOL," said O'Leary, a waggish, silk-voiced radio veteran who partnered with Don behind the mike at countless football and basketball games before retiring in the '90s. "Our group was all basically the same age – (Mary) Lou was a little younger. We'd usually go out to eat or just have a few drinks and talk. Those were good days."

O'Leary recalls seeing Mary Lou on the day she interviewed for the job. With her, also vying for the position, was a well-set female of prodigious physical stature.

"The guys in the office were calling her Boom-Boom," he said. "Mary Lou and Boom-Boom were waiting for the office manager to get back from lunch and do the interviews, but there was some sort of hang-up and the office manager didn't get back right away. So Boom-Boom took off. Mary Lou got the job – and everyone was happy that she did."

Don and Mary Lou's friendship gathered steam as they shared common interests.

"I think it helped that I'd always enjoyed sports," Mary Lou said. "I liked going to his games, and going out and getting a sandwich afterward. He played about every night of the week in the summer. And our group at the station bowled together, too, although Don and I bowled on different teams. Sports were something that we had in common and brought us together."

As for winning over Mary Lou's family, Don had a great head start. Her father was a good bowler who Don had seen before at the bowling alley.

Best of all, the force of an even greater common denominator was at work.

"My father was a White Sox fan," Mary Lou said. "He and Don got along well, naturally. I was a Sox fan, too."

Don and Mary Lou celebrated together when the Sox clinched the pennant, and commiserated together when they lost to the Dodgers in the World Series. It was a magical summer.

Don had had other girlfriends before but was never sold. Something about Mary Lou's unhurried serenity appealed to him. She was fun. She got his jokes. Where other girlfriends had applied the full-court press for marriage, Mary Lou seemed indifferent. She was having fun dating and voiced no particular desire to stampede to the altar. Maybe Don read her laissez-faire approach to the courtship as an inner strength that can be lethal to a guy laying his heart on the line. Perhaps he saw in her a relaxed assurance that if it didn't happen with him, it would happen somewhere else.

Whatever the dynamic, theirs was a bond Don did not want broken. Before long Mary Lou was convinced, too, that she'd found the one with whom she wanted to get on board.

"All the people at WJOL were kind of shocked when they heard," she recalls. "It was less than a year before it got serious. We tried to keep it quiet as best we could, and we did a pretty good job. We just played it cool. Everybody at the station got along and was involved with each other somehow. It wasn't that hard to do. There were just five ladies working there. I think some people knew, or suspected. But after nine months of dating, it was serious."

WJOL aired a segment on Saturday afternoons called Church Bells Ring, which announced social calendars and upcoming sermons at various local houses of worship.

On the afternoon of November 11, 1961, there came an announcement that undoubtedly raised some eyebrows among the listeners.

"We had guys who liked to kid around," said O'Leary, an Illinois Basketball Hall of Fame inductee and a blithe spirit who led the office in every category of mischief. "Whoever was on board that day would read the announcements, kind of solemn-like. We had a guy, a part-timer, reading them that day. Well, someone had stuck in the announcement that, 'The Russian Orthodox Church will hold baptismal services at the base of the Ruby Street Bridge.' An obvious joke, but the guy read it, word-for-word – and solemnly, like he was supposed to. It was one of the few times I wasn't involved in something like that. On Monday I was told, 'They want to see you in the office.' They asked me if I had anything to do with it, but I didn't. I didn't even know anything about it."

O'Leary had an airtight alibi. On that Saturday afternoon – a beautiful sunny day that gave way to rain later that night – he was at St. Mary's Carmelite Church, standing up in Don and Mary Lou's wedding.

"I was just on Cloud Nine that day," Mary Lou said. "Nothing bothered me. You go through the motions, actually, but it's just a very, very happy time to spend with your family and your friend. It was a special, special day."

The reception was at D'Amico's and there was a live band. Don and Mary Lou danced to the song "To Each His Own," and Chuck sat in on the drums.

"I'll never forget that day," Don said. "It was perfect."

The next morning they drove to New Orleans, where they spent two weeks relaxing, eating at nice restaurants and watching live shows, including one by Tony Bennett.

Don and Mary Lou favored the sultry climes for vacation spots – Punta Cana, Dominican Republic, Aruba, Hawaii, St. Martin's, Florida, Arizona – and would eventually buy a condo in Siesta Key near Sarasota. That summer home became a tropical haven that would be enjoyed by their kids and grandkids.

"It's been our sanctuary vacation spot," Sheri said. "My dad discovered it when he was in Sarasota covering the White Sox spring training one year. If he hadn't been there, we'd have never known what a beautiful and peaceful place that beach is. My dad went there as a young man, then he later went with my mom and then with us kids. When we were younger, we kids would go there for Spring Break with our friends – and then I went there as a newlywed, and now my kids go to that same beach. Talk about tradition!"

Throughout many of Don and Mary Lou's earlier holiday trips, the palm trees of Florida and the sun-baked Arizona desert provided beautiful scenery for what was ultimately another day at the office.

"We'd go to spring training every year for our vacation, but for Don it was a working vacation," Mary Lou said. "I knew his work was involved, but I didn't know how involved. I never thought it would hamper our relationship. I just didn't put it all together at first. We got invited to a lot of things. There was constant, constant involvement. It's been a fast-paced life, but very fun. We meet baseball fans, bowling fans and football fans, all different kinds of people at these functions. Every season was another sport, another banquet, another group of people. It was kind of hard going to the banquets at first because I didn't know many of them. But I made up my mind to get involved, and some of those people we've met are our dearest friends to this day."

Back on Joliet home turf, Don's reputation as a big name in local sports continued to grow. He was firmly entrenched in the "Big Three" – football, basketball and baseball – and had also made substantial inroads in the bowling and pool scene. The bigger he got, the bigger the names that turned up to do his show. Carmen Salvino and Don Carter were among his professional bowling guests.

"I had Willie Mosconi on once, one of the greatest pool players I've ever seen," Don said. "Big, gray-haired guy, and such a nice person."

A local player, Bob Brandolino, once ran 38 balls in a row in an exhibition match with Mosconi.

"Everyone was thinking he was going to beat the champ," Don said. "And then Willie ran about 100 straight. Man, that guy could play. I've never seen a guy get such good position from shot to shot. He was just an amazing player."

The match was held at a place called the Don Ladas Chalk and Cue and Archery Too. Earlier that year, Don bought the old Bowl Era bowling alley on Cass Street and with Chuck as his partner turned it into a 24-table pool hall, four-lane bowling alley and archery center. It was simply the place to be for those aspiring to be the next Willie Mosconi, Don Carter or Robin Hood.

That's to say, it *was* the place to be before he got the phone call.

"It was a Joliet Police officer named Lou Konich who gave me the news and I'll never forget how he put it," Don said. "It was 3 in the morning when the phone rang and after I picked it up and said hello Lou goes, 'Hey Don, your joint's on fire.' I hurried over there because I wanted to save a couple of things if I could. One was pretty special to me – a pool cue that a friend bought me in Greece when he was in the Navy. But they wouldn't let me go in. I just stood outside and watched as the building expanded and then exploded. I've never seen anything like it."

With the steady flow of upbeat, civil patrons and thriving league play, the Chalk and Cue was just too good a thing to give up on. Don bounced back from the fire loss and bought Bowl Era on Van Buren Street in what is now center field at Silver Cross Field. He and Chuck ran the place, as before, and kept the Chalk and Cue name for their new business.

White Sox infielder Pete Ward shot pool there, as did the guy who announced the Sox games, Red Rush.

"Red Rush was a really good pool player," Don said. "He and Ward got into a really long match one night – and Ward was pacing around, getting nervous because the Sox had a game at noon the next day. But they stayed there until it closed – 3 a.m. A lot of people stayed there until closing. We had a hard time getting them to leave at 3. It was a great situation. The police were really good about keeping an eye on it, and everyone had fun. We had some guys who could really play pool. Dizzy Trout was a very good pool player."

Mary Lou got in on the fun, too, teaming with Kathy Lenci to win first place in one of the women's summer leagues.

"It was probably a fluke that we won, but it was a lot of fun," she said. "I'm not a person who has to win all the time. We enjoyed ourselves, though. A lot of people enjoyed going to the Chalk and Cue."

A young daughter Sheri being one of them.

"I remember looking in awe at the archery section," she said. "It seemed as huge as McCormick Place to me at the time. I was only five years old, but I can remember the counter, the pool tables and the bowling. The one thing that was constant is how friendly everyone was. I remember my Uncle Chuck giving me coins for the candy machines – you know, the machines that gave you a handful of candy."

Chuck was always on hand to help keep things running smoothly at the Chalk and Cue, playing the role of enforcer when necessary. But he had a soft side that wasn't lost on his niece.

"He was my godfather," Sheri said. "For sure, he was the protective type, but there was a lot of love there, too. Once when I was a little girl at (St. Mary's Plainfield) school, we talked about guardian angels. My Uncle Chuck was the image that came to my mind, and what I believed got me through any time when I was scared."

Chuck and Don's spending time together was nothing new. As it was in the sandlot baseball games, the Sundays at the Princess Theater, the neighborhood brawls, the bike riding along the river walls and the nights talking about nothing and everything until they fell asleep, the brothers were always there for each other.

"We did everything together," Don said. "He was so much more than a brother to me."

Don and Chuck flourished as business partners at the Chalk and Cue until Chuck got sick. Although his brother and lifelong protector was dealing with lung cancer, it was still impossible for Don to imagine Chuck in a fight that he wouldn't win.

Cancer patients in the '70s did not yet have the benefit of targeted delivery mechanisms like linear accelerators. Treatments for the disease were crude by today's standards, and Chuck's condition continued to worsen. He flew to Arizona to see an oncologist, and after receiving word that he should return to Joliet, he died in the air, on a private plane, at the age of 47. It was a devastating loss for Don.

"My mom and dad did a good job of protecting us from the outside world, from anything that wasn't perfect and happy, as most parents do," Sheri said. "But that was a day that I still remember, even as little as I was. It was the first time I saw my dad cry."

"We were so close, Chuck and I," Don said. "I tried like crazy to get him to quit smoking. He told me at the end that he wished he'd listened. Back then only one out of 10 people with that type of cancer survived."

Thirty-three years after his brother's passing, Don still gets emotional recounting their times together at the billiard parlor.

"Chuck had settled down a lot in his adult years," he said. "He was a great guy, a good brother. He lost his wife Kay when she was 35, and that was when he got sick. Up till then, he was the enforcer at the Chalk and Cue. We ran a classy outfit – mirrors on the walls, rugs on the floor. We called it a billiard parlor, not a pool hall. Chuck ran the leagues, and we didn't take any garbage from anybody. If your place got a reputation as wild and wooly, your business would suffer. That's not the kind of parlor we wanted to have. We had a lot of leagues, and everyone followed the rules. We gave kids three opportunities; if they screwed up three times, they were out of there.

"One kid started crying after we barred him. We told him we didn't need his business if he was going to start trouble. He said he had no home. He begged us not to bar him. So we stuck with him, and he never acted up again. Parents used to drop their kids off on Sundays because they knew they were in good hands. If anyone started trouble, Chuck would take them outside and deal with them."

In the aftermath of having lost his older brother and closest friend, Don was faced with another big decision: to keep his bowling alley or the radio job.

Business was in his blood like bowling was, but in the end it wasn't too tough a call to make.

"I couldn't be cooped up," he said. "I had to keep the job at WJOL. I just enjoyed the change of sports seasons and being around people. Who would work for 54 years at one place? Who is that nuts? But I've enjoyed it. It's been fun."

Kissing goodbye his position as a public figure would have not only cooped up Don's free spirit. It would have also denied him a bird's-eye view of some great games, and meeting some exceptional people.

Joliet Catholic High School won its fifth state title under coach Gordie Gillespie with an 8-7 win over Deerfield in the 1981 championship game. The final score was notable in that it typified the attitude that Gillespie's teams had throughout 26 straight winning seasons.

Gordie went for two points after a touchdown instead of the high-percentage one-point kick for the same reason he seldom deigned to punt on fourth-and-three: He knew his offense would make those yards, and he knew that his players knew it, too.

Of the many sports luminaries whose paths Don has crossed, none has cast a longer shadow on the Joliet area than Gordon Gillespie.

A powerful motivator and a tactician of surpassing genius, Gillespie began his coaching career in 1950, coaching baseball, football and basketball with a dynamism reminiscent of John McGraw, Don Shula and Johnny Wooden. His renown is such that only his first name is required to reference him; when folks in the Joliet area speak of Gordie, they don't mean Gordie Howe.

In addition to leading Joliet Catholic to five state football championships, Gordie also won three National Association of Intercollegiate Athletics baseball titles – two while coaching Lewis College and one with the University of St. Francis. He was just the second coach in college baseball to win 1,500 games, and his teams have won 22 Chicagoland Collegiate Athletic Conference titles. In 1998 he was named "Coach of the Century" by Collegiate Baseball Magazine. Fifty-seven baseball players he coached went on to sign professional contracts.

Gillespie, who coached men's basketball at Lewis and women's basketball at St. Francis, played under Ray Meyer at DePaul University and turned down an offer from the NBA Rochester Royals in order to teach and coach. A member of 13 Halls of Fame, Gordie was named the coach of the "All-Time Illinois High School Football Team" by the Chicago Tribune. He has achieved so much throughout his career that it's a shorter job to list the awards he hasn't won.

Feel free to assume that a coach of his import has a good handle on the psychology of an athlete.

"Don was a very competitive athlete himself," Gillespie said. "Whether it was softball or racquetball, whatever he did, he tried to maximize what he was about, in the sense of giving your all, doing your all, playing hard, playing fair and playing honest. If ever there was a gentleman who typified Joliet sports, that was Don."

It takes one to know one. Gordie was as hard-nosed and demanding as you might expect of a coach of his caliber. He's also a very nice guy, a gentleman, and the respect Don and he share is mutual.

"Don Ladas is WJOL," Gordie said. "In the years I've been here, there's always been Don Ladas connected with the broadcast of various events, whether it was football, baseball or bowling. He did everything, all the hard jobs. He took great pride in what he did. Every bowler he talked with on his bowling show, you thought that bowler was the No. 1 bowler in country. If you were a golfer, you felt like you were Tiger Woods. No matter what he broadcast, he brought out the best in the team, the coaching. He never thrived on the negative. While a lot of the press today will always try to find fault with people, Don Ladas found goodness in all facets of sports. And he hasn't changed. If he comments on a play when he's doing football, he never cheapens the atmosphere."

Gordie and Don both look back fondly on the days before sports media evolved a more critical eye.

"In athletics today, a lot of people are looking for the bizarre story, the ones that hurt people," he said. "That was never Don Ladas. He always built people up, in the nicest kind of way, and he was always very, very informed. If he didn't have anything good to say about you, or about an incident, he wouldn't say anything at all. He never tore down anybody; he always tried to build people up. He's always positive. You were always glad to be around. He doesn't like to talk about himself. He wants to talk about what you're doing."

Having competed on a high level himself, Gillespie has known the full spectrum of emotions that all athletes will eventually countenance. Gordie may never have missed the head pin in the 10th frame of a perfect game, but he is nonetheless fluent in both the thrill of victory and the agony of defeat.

"I don't look at Don as a Harry Caray kind of personality, a guy who wouldn't always be kind," he said. "In other words, if I'm at the plate and I strike out for the fourth time in the game, Harry would say, 'He couldn't hit it with a washboard.' That wasn't Don Ladas. If you got struck out four times, he'd praise the pitcher.

"To me, when you speak of Don Ladas, you speak of a gentleman. They're synonymous. That's what he is, that's who is he, that's what he's been. If anybody has maximized the Joliet sports scene, he's the one who's done it. He's always had positive things to say about the various programs, always praising the Joliet athletes for what they are. Joliet is a mill town. Joliet is a tough guy town. Joliet is a town where you have a great mixture of people, whether it's black, Mexican, Polish, original Slovaks, whatever. In all the various neighborhoods, Don's the kind of guy who will be accepted anywhere because of who he is and what he stands for. He's for fair play all the time. I don't know of a finer gentleman in the sports broadcasting scene. He made a lot of people feel good about themselves. If my bowling average was 101, Don would make me feel like my average was 250.

"He's just a class act. He's the kind of guy I'd do anything for. You don't want to do Don Ladas a favor because he might say your name on the radio. You want to do a favor for Don Ladas because you love him. That's the way I feel about him.

He's always building up someone else. He'd never build up a shady character. He wouldn't blast him either. He just wouldn't mention him. In my early days here, the '60s, '70s and '80s, you know what you were going to get on game day. We might not have been the best team, but one thing we did know is we were going to give 100 percent effort. And I think that's true with Don. With him, you're going to get the very best. Whether he's doing a bowling show or a marble contest, you'd think he was calling a World Series game."

Announcers back in the 1950s and '60s employed a vernacular that has been described as everything from colorful to cornball. A free throw in basketball was shot from the "charity stripe," and baseball's inning was often referred to as a "stanza." The guys behind the mike often heaped effusive praise on the competitors and rarely took potshots at their performance or effort. The style suited Don during those early broadcasts, and he stuck with it.

"Batters are holding a shillelagh, pitchers are throwing an apple over the platter," said Scott Slocum, the station program director and sports director who joined Don at WJOL in the summer of 1987. "He still does the same stuff. Sometimes if we have a new guy in the booth who hasn't worked with Don, he'll turn around and have this puzzled look. Then I'll tell him Don's talking about a bat and ball.

"Anybody who has been doing one thing, and has been accepted and appreciated for as long as Don has, has to be given all the respect in the world. I came to WJOL right out of college. I was a kid. I immediately had a ton of respect for him,

Don Ladas (right), with former Los Angeles Dodgers manager Tom Lasorda (center), and former major league pitcher Tom Brennan at the Will County Old Timers Baseball Association banquet.

Don Ladas with Will County Executive Larry Walsh at Silver Cross Field before the inaugural Joliet Jackhammers baseball game

Don and Scott Slocum calling a basketball game

Detroit Tigers pitcher Bill Gullickson (center) with Don and veteran sportswriter Bill Gleason (right) in the locker room at Comiskey Park

Don Ladas and former major league baseball player Ron Coomer in the press box at the Wish Upon A Star Softball In The Snow benefit game

Don and former New York Yankees and Chicago White Sox first baseman Bill "Moose" Skowron at the Old Timers banquet

Don (foreground) listens to St. Louis Cardinals Hall of Famer Stan Musial at the Will County Old Timers Baseball Association banquet

Major league pitcher Chris Michalak

Don Ladas has been inducted into nine Halls of Fame throughout his 54-year career at WJOL

Don Ladas hitting a line drive in a 16-inch softball game.

The Ladas family -- (front) Mary Lou, Don and Angie; (back) Don Jr. and Sheri

just looking at his resume. Everywhere in town I went, it was Don-this and Don-that. If I walked into a gym without him, it would be, 'Where's Ladas?' 'Why are you here and not Don?'"

Slocum proved to be an able protégé, and has represented the station with a level of industry and professionalism that reflects well on the guy who showed him the ropes. Don and he complement one another nicely on the air, and for the past two decades-plus the tandem has been admirable in promoting high school and college athletics in the Joliet area. Slocum demonstrated a knack for innovation and a keen eye for marketing, establishing a popular preseason high school basketball tournament that bears the station's name, and later adding another WJOL-sponsored preseason high school tournament – baseball – to the community mix. The preseason baseball tournament will forever hold special significance for Don. More on that a little later.

By the time Slocum broke into the medium 21 years ago, it had already undergone dramatic changes from the crackerjack, gee-whiz days of yore.

With the advent of cable TV in the mid-1970s came a proliferation of media, and a subsequent increase in competition for listeners, viewers and readers. Gradually, announcing styles changed, owing to the national zeitgeist and the need to distinguish oneself among the sudden crush of media on the scene. Merely reciting the runs, hits and errors could no longer guarantee a loyal audience and advertiser-friendly numbers. A unique and beguiling delivery was also becoming required fare. The Entertainment and Sports Programming Network would later set the bar for clever sound bites and hip catchphrases, and has figured heavily in the absorption of sports lingo into everyday terminology.

Don doesn't do "boo-yah!" He won't bark like a cocker spaniel when a running back "Could! Go! All! The! Way!" He just refuses to swing the spotlight in his direction. The way he sees it, in today's sports panorama there are too many stars and not enough sky.

"I've always thought that the game is the story, and the ones playing are the story," he said. "The announcers are not the story."

The success of ESPN may have hastened the idea of media personalities as showcase entities, but the messenger had begun to take center stage earlier in the decade.

You say you want a revolution?

There was a sea change in America in the early 1970s. The country was riven by the Vietnam War, divided into factions of "establishment" and "anti-establishment" – or "rednecks" and "peace creeps," depending on your view of the war and how strongly you felt about it.

Also afoot was a paradigm shift in journalism. When Bob Woodward and Carl Bernstein dug through the scandal that unraveled Richard Nixon's presidency, the power of the press was center stage as seldom before. A new journalistic template took shape, as vanguards of the fourth estate morphed from watch dogs to attack dogs.

The siege mentality soon bled into sports journalism. A dynamic took root whereby the seriousness of a sportswriter was measured by the enmity with which he called or wrote about the games he covered. One Chicago daily paper in the '70s employed a columnist whose reputation as a "ripper" was so notorious that the paper showcased him in a radio advertisement. In the ad, players were depicted as shaking with fear upon seeing before the start of the game that "he" was there covering it, and that reproach and humiliation were sure to follow.

"To me, when Woodward and Bernstein wrote about Watergate, that, in a way, changed the face of journalism in America," University of St. Francis basketball coach Pat Sullivan said. "Everybody became an investigative reporter. Think about the protection that Babe Ruth and President Kennedy got for their little peccadilloes. Then all of a sudden, journalism turned 180 degrees. When sports journalism turned to investigative reporting, and you weren't putting enough dirt out on people, you weren't doing your job."

Sullivan was captain of the Joliet Catholic basketball team in the early '60s when he first met Don in a post-game interview.

"I can't remember the game or who we played or the situation or why he interviewed me," Sullivan said. "But I do remember this, and I think it's symbolic and indicative of who Don Ladas is. I'm a 17-year-old senior, and I remember … his kindness. Now, isn't that something? Isn't that interesting that I remember his kindness?"

As a globe-trotting basketball instructor who conducted camps in Belgium, Greece and Ireland, Sullivan noted how deeply acts of kindness are received when one is operating out of his or her element. As a high school senior who had never been on the radio before, Sullivan was out of his comfort zone but remembers clearly how Don had made him feel at ease.

"You really do remember acts of kindness no matter where you are," he said. "Now, how about the great part. At 64 years old, I can say that Don Ladas has never changed that modus operandi. I think that's why he's held in such high esteem by those of us in the coaching profession."

Sullivan echoes Don's credo of life: It's a team sport and everyone's playing.

"Don never embarrassed the kids or coaches," he said. "We all make stupid decisions. I may lead the league in that. You appreciate people who don't harp on mistakes or emphasize the negative. That's what Don has done. He's never forgotten that it's a game. Like Gordie says, 'Do you think a guy strikes out because he wants to, or that he throws the potential game-ending out over the first baseman's head because he wants to?'

"The field of cybernetics holds that we tend to remember our mistakes more than we remember our successes. Don never lost sight of the fact that it is a game, and at the collegiate and high school game, we're not talking pro athlete. We're talking about kids playing and giving everything they have because they love it. I think that's why everyone, players and coaches, have always held Don in the highest of regard, because he understood."

Don notched his fair share of game-winning hits and bases-clearing doubles, but he's also booted a few grounders over the years. His bowling average has been consistently around 180 all his adult life. He once took a perfect game into the 10th frame.

"As a coach, when I see a kid throw a ball away at the end of a game, I've been that kid," Sullivan said. "When he misses a free throw at the end, I've missed that free throw. I was Gordie's captain and I got beat (pitching in a baseball game with Lewis College) that would've sent us back to our third national championship. You can never forget what it feels like when you make an error that might cost a game. Maybe it's because Don Ladas continued to compete – he was a helluva racquetball player – that he remembers how lousy it feels when you don't help your team."

Don holds certain things in baseball as sacrosanct. Running onto and off of the field is one, and wearing your game face is another. Putting out the effort every moment you're on the field. Even when age began taking a toll on his body, and leg doubles at the softball benefits had become leisurely one-base hits, Don's respect for clean, hard competition never wavered.

"The moniker for Joliet is 'City of Champions,' which started with the American Legion band and all the championships they had," Sullivan said. "Now when you think back to it, when you go back to Ed Spiezio and those guys winning the national championships for Pony League, what's the one constant throughout all the championships? It's been Don Ladas. He either broadcasted the actual game, or when people came home from their games, it was Don who made sure that their success was promulgated throughout the community. His recollection of games and the people who played them – the down, the yardage situation, the time left in the game – it's encyclopedic in nature."

Sullivan lauds Don's choice of staying positive throughout a career whose parameters shifted so dramatically.

"It was the same sort of dynamic working with coaching," Sullivan said. "You could either decide, 'I'm going to try to get the kids to graduate and we're going to win with that paradigm,' or, 'I don't give a darn if they graduate, I want them in here and I want to win.' Everyone has to make a decision on that, and that's why, thank God, Don Ladas made the decision he made."

Sullivan recalled being asked on the radio about one of his players being busted for cocaine possession. It was the first Sullivan had heard of it.

"Don would never have surprised me on the air like that," Sullivan said. "He'd have asked me about it off the air, and even at that his reaction would have been, 'I can't believe that happened, he's such a good kid,' or something like that. As it turned out, we dealt with the situation, the kid admitted his coke habit and he got help. Today he's the vice president of a company."

A contentious media driven by a "gotcha" mentality had grown in size and ferocity through the '70s and into the '80s, with the tabloid press' hypercritical eye lamented in popular songs by Don Henley ("Dirty Laundry") and George Harrison ("Devil's Radio").

Soon there was court TV broadcasting to the nation the worst moments in some poor shlub's life. Football may have leapfrogged baseball as America's sport, but both took a back seat to the new national pastime of voyeurism. No fall from grace was too juicy to jump all over with both feet, and the bigger the name, the better. The same agencies that dutifully hyped and hoisted the careers of young entertainers, politicians and sports figures were every bit if not more enthusiastic in charting their inevitable plummet back to earth.

There was also a sea change at the Ladas household in 1970. Don and Mary Lou welcomed their first child, Sheri, and the home that was warm and loving instantly became something far more special. Angie and Don Jr.'s arrival two and four years later, respectively, were the pieces that made the picture whole.

"Yeah, that changed me, alright," Don said. "I was so happy. My kids mean everything to me."

So do the memories of their infancy – Sheri's first steps, Angie's first words and Donnie's first base hit with a Wiffle ball. Even after the longest day at the office, it was always a good drive home for Don, knowing what was there waiting for him.

"When they're young like that, it's such a great thing," Don said. "I loved being a dad."

The days at home with his wife and kids were the best. When one of them fell ill, it was the worst.

"Sheri had a heart problem when she was two-and-a-half," Don said. "There was a hole in it, and she had an operation. Talk about a helpless feeling. Seeing her in the hospital like that, getting ready for surgery, it tore me up. It was the worst few days of my life, not knowing how she was going to do. Afterward, when she made it through, it was such a huge relief. I'd never been happier."

From the time he waved a U.S. flag in the middle of the ring after winning the gold medal in the 1968 Olympics until the time he regained the world heavyweight boxing title at the age of 45, George Foreman was a favorite of mainstream America.

He cashed in on his popularity. After becoming the oldest man ever to win a major heavyweight title, he went on to the business world, where he landed an entrepreneurial haymaker with his novel, grease-draining electric grill that "knocks out the fat" in hamburgers and steaks.

En route to his Olympic conquest, Foreman got knocked on his USDA prime hind-quarters by Billy Boy Thompson.

Thompson is a Joliet native who not only gave Foreman a good challenge in their '68 Olympics Trial match, but who also defeated Ron Lyle to win the 1970 National Gold Gloves heavyweight title. Lyle later turned pro and fought in title bouts against Foreman and Muhammad Ali.

At six feet and 180 pounds, Thompson may have been better suited for the light heavyweight division. While there was always some dispute about which was his ideal weight class, there was never a doubt that you didn't want him hitting you.

"Billy Boy had me rolling," Foreman said. "Boy, did he hit me hard."

Thompson won the Catholic Youth Organization heavyweight title in the mid-'60s and took off from there, racking up five Golden Gloves titles, three Illinois state title belts and earning the No. 1 U.S. heavyweight amateur rank by the Amateur Boxing Association.

His road to renown was well-tracked in Joliet.

Don's father Gus trained fighters, and ran a boxing ring in the third-floor upstairs of his restaurant that held 200 people. Don's background in the sport and his immersion in the local sports community locked up a lasting friendship with Billy Boy.

"He's been a savior," Thompson said. "Not just to me, but to so many other athletes in this area. He's been the mouthpiece for so many of us. I wouldn't have been as well-known as I had if it wasn't for Don Ladas."

Thompson was a high school junior when Don interviewed him at the Peter Claver Center in downtown Joliet. Billy Boy would later go on to become an all-conference defensive end at Joliet Junior College, but when he first stepped into a ring it was clear that boxing was his calling.

"During the interview, he was more like a friend," Thompson said. "He got to the point, and it seemed like he cared about you. He wanted me to do well where I was at. He was very direct, very concerned. I had no idea it was going be an everlasting relationship with him, but it was, especially when I started progressing in boxing. He interviewed me in football, too. I saw him at a lot of events. He covered a lot of things."

And he's covered them in some shaky places. He's done basketball games in tiny gyms with lousy acoustics and hostile crowds. He and Frank O'Leary once called a football game from a piece of scaffolding behind a makeshift desk, with their feet and legs dangling 60 feet from the ground.

But nothing compared to the vibe in the air at Stateville Prison, where Don covered the fight between Billy Boy Thompson and inmate Floyd "Jumbo" Cummings.

"The warden told me that all the prisoners would be asking me to help get them out," Don said. "He said they were all going to say they weren't guilty, and to ask if I had any influence in getting them out. I walked through there and sure enough, some of the guys started telling me right away that they weren't guilty, and asked if I could get them out. I said I'd see what I could do."

At 6-foot-3 and 240 well-sculpted pounds, it was clear that Cummings took advantage of the prison weight room. Cummings also had an impressive body of work: he would fight Joe Frazier to a draw, and nearly knock out heavyweight champion James "Bonecrusher" Smith in the first round of their fight that Smith eventually won by decision. The chatter about how badly Cummings would beat Thompson had begun shortly after the fight was first announced, and had hit a crescendo by the time Don and Billy Boy walked into Stateville.

"Don was kind of nervous, but he was pretty cool," Billy Boy said. "That was a good fight. Everyone said Cummings was going to kill me. I said, 'No way – I walked into this prison on my own and I'll walk out on my own.' Getting beaten up or knocked out was the least of my worries. George Formean said the same thing. Ron Lyle said the same thing. Anywhere you go, you might find a fighter talking smack. I said that whenever that bell rings, then we'll find out who's gonna go somewhere."

No one was killed, or even knocked out. But Cummings was awarded the decision.

"I thought I won the fight," Billy Boy said. "Don did too. Afterward I turned to him and said, 'Don, did he kill me? Did he kill me, Don?'"

It was one of just 10 defeats suffered by Thompson, who knocked out 95 opponents in 125 fights. The most notable of those bouts was the Foreman fight in the finals of the Olympic Trials.

"I'd fought him the year before," Thompson recalled. "You see a lot of fighters and you remember faces. You don't always know who you're going to fight. I knew he'd knocked out a bunch of fighters, but I didn't think anybody could beat me in 1968.

"I looked across the ring and I saw this big guy, this big, strong guy jumping up and down like a kangaroo. I'd seen him fight in other fights – he was big and strong and young but … I won't say he was slow because when you're 18 years old, you're still fast. Youth will carry you a long way, right? I knocked him down in the first round with a straight right hand. I thought I had him, but somehow he survived the punch. I tried to catch him again with another right hand but I couldn't catch him. He got back up on his own. By the third round I thought I had him, but I figured I had to knock him out. All of a sudden he caught me on the jaw with a crushing right hand I thought, 'Oh man, he's gonna knock me out.' I tried to go down as fast as I could because when you're helpless like that guys will take advantage of you. He swung a wild right hand and I was trying to fall as fast as I could. I could feel the breeze of the punch missing me and I was like, 'Man, this guy's trying to kill me!'

"Anyway, I thought I was OK when I got up. I thought I was fine. The ref asked me how many fingers he was holding up, what day it was, that kind of thing. I said I was OK but he said no and stopped the fight. In dressing room, Foreman came up and said, 'Man, you hit hard.' I said, 'You hit pretty hard yourself.' I don't think I would've won the fight if they hadn't stopped it. I was going for the knockout and not the decision. I called Don Ladas up and we talked about it on the air. George

Foreman wasn't a big deal back then so it wasn't as big of news as it would turn out to be."

Thompson saw Foreman one other time, when Thompson was winning the National Golden Gloves heavyweight title in Las Vegas.

"Joe Frazier and Joe Louis were there, too," Billy Boy said. "I was in heaven.

"Of course, I'd be on the phone talking with Don about it afterward. He'd always tell me to call him collect, to be sure to please call him collect and let him know. Don was involved not just with Billy Boy Thompson, but all kinds of stuff. He is the voice of Joliet. All the good sports memories I have, Don was always there, whether it was tournament or just a show fight. He always kept us out there in public eye. Whatever it was, he always played a big part in my life."

For his part, Don is a lover and not a fighter. But cross him at your own risk.

"I saw Don deck one of the guys at the station," Slocum recalls. "They got in an argument and they went outside. There were two hits – Don hitting him, and him hitting the ground. For as sweet as he is, Don's a tough guy. He's a tough Greek. He won't put up with anything from anyone. We were doing a game at (New Lenox) Lincoln-Way and he almost got in a fight with a fan. The fan came up and got in his face and they almost went at it."

Billy Boy appreciated Don's dedication and style, and once asked him whether he considered moving on to greener pastures.

"I said to him, 'Don I've been all over the U.S. and I've seen a lot of announcers. Why have you never left Joliet?'" Thompson said. "He could've made it in New York or L.A., I know he could've. Once you've got a good name for yourself and you know the sports, you can get a break here or there to get that big job. He said, 'I just love Joliet.' That's what he said."

Tom Thayer is revered in Joliet not only because he was a fixture on the most dominant sports team in Chicago history. Thayer is loved because throughout the stratospheric highs of the 1985 Super Bowl season with the Bears he never lost the common touch.

An offensive lineman who played on two of Gordie's state-championship teams at Joliet Catholic, Thayer made All-American at Notre Dame before playing two years in the old United States Football League. His coach was George Allen, who once talked about Thayer during a post-practice jog with a hustling radio reporter from Joliet.

"I remember working out at the YMCA when I was younger, and I'd see Don Ladas playing racquetball there," Thayer said. "It was always a good thing – it pumped you up to have him see you work out."

Thayer gained his starting job in the third game of the '85 season, when Kurt Becker went out with an injury. The Bears trailed the Vikings 21-9 in that Thursday night game in Minnesota before rallying furiously to win 33-24.

What followed is classic Chicago sports lore. The Bears drubbed the defending champion 49ers on the road and pole-axed the Cowboys in Dallas en route to a 15-1 regular season that preceded three playoff blowouts and the franchise's first Super Bowl title.

"You could tell in his high school games that Tom was going to be a special player," Don said. "He was quick, strong and smart, and nobody outworked him. His brother Rick was a great football player, too – a big, strong fullback."

Thayer was underrated on the Bears. Agile, heady and the strongest guy on a team full of heavyweight titans, he played a stretch of 53 straight games without a holding penalty, an amazing feat for an offensive lineman.

"I didn't know about that streak until I saw it on the back of one of my football cards," Thayer said. "When I finally got one, it was just me being lazy. You don't even think about the games when you didn't get a holding penalty – you think about the one that ended the streak."

With two marquee names already on the offensive line – Jim Covert and Jay Hilgenberg – and a parade of defensive players garnering honors, Thayer was passed up for the Pro Bowl consideration that he surely would have had on virtually any other team.

While his skills as an offensive guard may have been underappreciated, there is no hiding his talent in the radio booth. Thayer has been a gold mine of insight as an analyst for the Bears over the past 10 seasons. His ability to identify the action on the field and delineate it into lay terms has made him one of the best color announcers in the game. Thayer would bring much to the table if he ever pursued a network job.

But he's not interested. Like his radio counterpart in Joliet, Thayer is exactly where he wants to be.

"It's great if people like the job I'm doing," he said. "I know I've enjoyed it a lot, and I don't want to go anywhere else. If

I'm fortunate enough to be able to finish my career doing Bears games, that's what I want to do."

There are various schools of thought on advancing up the occupational ladder, the most prominent being that one should keep reaching higher until they've achieved that which is considered the top of their profession.

But happiness does not appear on a pay stub. And as many successful television actors who fell on their face trying their luck on the big screen know, sometimes the best situation is the one right in front of you.

As was eloquently postulated in the Peter Principal, "In a hierarchy every employee tends to rise to his level of incompetence."

Or, as was put not quite as elegantly in an old Haitian proverb, "The higher a monkey climbs, the more you see his ass."

Joliet and Chicago will always be fine with Thayer, and Don can relate.

"I never felt the need to go on to something bigger and better," Don said, "because I never thought there was anything bigger or better than what I had here."

"Joliet has been lucky to have him," Thayer said.

If you wanted to know why your favorite high school team ran a draw play on third-and-20, or why they left their stud in the game with four fouls in the third quarter, you tuned into to Coaches Corner.

The weekly show broadcast live at Al's Steak House was a huge hit, because it picked up where the postgame interviews left off and the host had a seamless way of pulling it all together.

One of the better shows featured Gordie Gillespie and Bill Zimmer, the Lockport High School football coach whose teams waged epic battles with Gillespie's at Joliet Catholic.

"I thought they were bitter enemies," Don said. "But when you get guys together over a few beers – although Gordie didn't drink – when you bring them together in a civil environment like that, it's a good thing. A lot of fans and families came out. Al said we could do the show there as long as we wanted."

Coaches Corner brought in the big names to talk about the big games.

"Coaches loved to talk about what happened to them in a game. If they won, they'd tell you what a good job they did, and if they lost they'd tell you what a lousy job their players did," Bob Basarich said.

Basarich was the basketball coach at Lockport in 1978, when his team, led by center Scott Parzych, completed a 33-0 season with a state-title win over Westchester St. Joseph.

St. Joe's advanced to the final on the legs of guard Isiah Thomas, who went on to play on Indiana University's 1981 national championship team, and was an NBA all-star who led the Detroit Pistons to back-to-back crowns in '89 and '90.

"We didn't have any special plans to stop Thomas in that game because we played a 1-3-1 matchup with all kinds of twists to it," Basarich said.

"St. Joe's did us a favor by beating (Chicago) Westinghouse. That team had Mark Aguirre, Skip Dillard and Bernard Randolph. All three of them played on those good DePaul teams

The Voice Of Joliet

after high school, and of course Aguirre was a very good player in the NBA. Beating Westinghouse might've taken something out of St. Joe's. We caught them at the right time."

Lockport had a 25th year anniversary celebration for that team, and another banquet honoring the top 50 players in school history. Don spoke at both functions.

"He was always a positive person who treated everyone with respect," Basarich said. "I remember some interviews after we lost a game. I'd come out of that locker room thinking we'd won. Don Ladas just talked me into how good we were.

"I wonder if he has any enemies. How can you get mad at a person who's never said anything bad about you or your program? He is the legend and the icon of the Joliet area. He can't help it if he's a White Sox fan."

Don has long touted the phenomenon of Joliet's disproportionately high number of premier athletes. It's no brag, just fact. A good indicator of that depth of talent was a baseball game between Joliet Central and Joliet Catholic in the spring of 1977.

The scouts had come out to watch Bill Gullickson pitch for Catholic High, which was understandable given Gullickson's 24-1 record over his last two years of high school. "Gully" also had thrown six no-hitters, but the number that most interested the scouts was the 93-mph clocked on his fastball.

Don, who of course covered the game, already knew Gullickson. He'd seen the potential in the big kid when he was piling up the strikeouts in the Belmont Little League.

"You could tell right there, with his size and the way he threw the ball, that he had the potential to make it to the major leagues," Don said.

Don was there when Gullickson was a 12-year-old mowing down overmatched batters, and he was there when Gully was an ambitious 14-year-old mowing his lawn. They lived in the same neighborhood, and Don paid the young pitcher with tickets to White Sox games.

"It was great," Gullickson said. "It was better than getting money."

Gully won his game against Joliet Central, which was expected. The surprise for the scouts came when a wiry kid from Central got around on one of Gullickson's fastballs.

Jesse Barfield, who Don also covered in the Belmont Little League when Barfield was a skinny kid batting seventh in the order, hit a shot off Gullickson so vicious that it literally broke a hole in the left-field picket fence. It was a ground rule double, but that two-bagger went a long way for Barfield. He was drafted in the ninth round by the Toronto Blue Jays that summer, and his 12-year major league career with the Jays and the New York Yankees included two Gold Gloves and a 40-home run season, most in the big leagues in 1986.

"I remember Don from when I was a kid, and I remember him interviewing us when we were in high school," said Barfield, whose son Josh now plays with the Cleveland Indians. "Don would always tell us that Joliet is the city of champions, and that we're counting on you. He'd always let you know he was in your corner. City of champions, I'd always think about that. There have been a lot of great athletes that came out of Joliet."

By the time the Blue Jays had grabbed Barfield in the draft, Gullickson was long gone. He was picked by the Montreal Expos in the first round and No. 2 overall behind Harold Baines of the White Sox.

Gullickson broke into the majors in 1980 and made an instant splash, putting together a 10-5 season that included an 18-strikeout game against the Cubs. It was the strikeout record for a rookie that stood until Kerry Wood broke it in 1998.

"That game was in Montreal, so I didn't see many people from Chicago or Joliet at the time," Gullickson said. "But when we came to Chicago, somehow I would run into Don Ladas and I was always thrilled to talk to him. It was never one of those, 'Let me hurry and get this done.' It was always … it was always more of an honor for me to do an interview with him."

Like many kids who grew up in the era before FM radio became en vogue, Gullickson remembers Don reading the bowling scores on WJOL.

"And I remember him announcing my games in Little League," he said. "Don was always a gentleman, always polite. I didn't know this when I was in Little League, but I realized it after I'd been exposed to more stuff as I grew up. He always wanted to know a good story, a refreshing, honest story. He never cared about the bad stuff. He was always a positive, truthful guy. When I think of it, he's been doing this all my life."

Gullickson pitched for two years in Japan before returning to finish his major league career with 162 victories, including 20 in the 1991 season for the Detroit Tigers. By that time he'd played with the Expos, Cincinnati Reds, New York Yankees and Yomiuri Giants. He'd dealt with the full spectrum of media reps.

"I ran into (journalists) who wanted to get a story that nobody else got, or something that could maybe further their career," Gullickson said. "But with Don, it was, 'I want to know the apple pie of the world.'

"You had to be careful with guys in the media because you didn't know if they were asking a question to get that answer, or to find out something else. So you sort of built up a little wall against it. And it's bad because not every apple in the bunch is a bad apple. But even if it's just one apple, then you've got to check all the apples."

Gullickson was the guest speaker at the 59th annual Old Timers Baseball Association of Will County banquet early in 2008. Don was the emcee. Gullickson was mingling with friends and hadn't gone in the main banquet room yet when he heard the voice.

"I heard him talking and I stopped and said, 'That's Don Ladas.' I don't know if you could say he's made a contribution to the Joliet sports community – he *is* the Joliet sports community. He didn't really contribute, he built it. He goes back to guys who are now 60 or 70 years old. He's always been sharp and on the ball and can recall stories from way back. Like I said, it was a thrill for me to do an interview with Don Ladas," he said.

The third party in the Joliet Catholic-vs.-Joliet Central drama was the guy catching Gullickson's speedball. Rick Colbert's quickness behind the plate and his ability to block the 90-mph sliders made a nice complement for his strong throwing arm and lively bat.

"Peripherally, I knew there were scouts in the stands," Colbert said. "I don't think Jesse or I knew we were being scouted. We figured they were there for Gully, and that was right because he was the king. We weren't savvy enough at that time to know that scouts might recommend you to colleges and so forth. We were real ham-and-eggers back then. Kids now, they're on the Internet, they know how things work, how a recommendation from a scout can help get you a scholarship.

"But back then we were just playing baseball, trying to beat each other for bragging rights. I weighed 168 and Jesse weighed 170. We were a couple of skinny kids who didn't even know where we going to college or anything like that. I think that game really helped Jesse out from what I understand. Scouts were watching Gully, and then they saw this skinny kid at Joliet Central who could roll the pole and get it there in time on a guy who's throwing over 90. They saw me catching a guy who's throwing 90 and has a great hook, and nothing is getting by me and I'm blocking everything. The impact of that day was big for both Jesse and me, and we didn't even know it."

Colbert was drafted by Minnesota and spent 17 years in professional ball as a player with the Twins, the Houston Astros, the Boston Red Sox and the St. Louis Cardinals organizations. Colbert also managed in the St. Louis organization, giving him an added perspective on the media.

"Probably the biggest compliment I can ever give Don is that having been in pro baseball, you're exposed to lot of different media," he said. "A lot of writers would be jumping on the negativity, the bad play, writing some sort of negative stuff to get themselves to the next level. Don was always above that; he always looked on the bright part of a performance. He always downplayed when someone didn't do so well or said something they shouldn't have said and he never concentrated on the negative. I can tell you, after 17 years in pro baseball as a player and manager, when I had to answer the questions after the games, I ran into a lot of jackasses. I really did. Guys who were trying to catch you, try to make you look stupid, sell a newspaper. Everything now is about what people have done wrong in a past life, if they're liars, something negative to bring up about somebody because people listen to that stuff. Don Ladas, all these years, has never done that.

"There's a bigger lesson from this guy. It's a real lousy place nowadays. It's dirty laundry. Don did not engage in dirty laundry, and because of that he's a well-loved man and respected in the media. There's more than enough inspiration from Don's life. He went the totally opposite way that everybody else has."

Colbert also played in the Belmont Little League, and was aware of the auspicious air the day took on when WJOL had their guy out covering the game.

"When we saw him coming to cover our games, it was huge," he said. "That's the first memory I have about him being there, that it was an important thing. That added to the drama for what we were doing as little guys. It made me want to do more, to succeed, to be more often in that position where I'm competing and everybody is watching or listening. Don was the first guy I remember who brought that to my baseball life."

Colbert's memories of the voice date back to a time before he had taken his first cut in Little League.

"Everybody had WJOL on when we were kids," he said. "We had him on the car radio, because back then AM radio was it. Every morning I woke up, I didn't even know who he was,

The Voice Of Joliet

he was doing Ten Pin Topics. I lived over on Washington Street. The first thing my mom did in the morning besides making coffee was turn on the radio. And he was there. He was always there. He's like the background of my life."

Colbert played with and against Don in several of the benefit softball games in Joliet.

"Don would be the manager of one of the teams, and every year the teams were called something different, depending on which pros were there playing," he said. "One year it was the Cubs and Sox and obviously Don had the Sox. He was really bearing down trying to win that game. He said, 'Rick, we've got a 13-run lead but I'm not giving this away.' I said, 'Don, you've got to get some of these other guys in the game or they're going to be mad.' He's something else. He really wants to win."

High school basketball ball devotees around Illinois got their first look at Roger Powell during the 1970 edition of March Madness.

Powell was only a sophomore at Joliet Central, but he was a man among boys. At 6-foot-5, he had good quickness and great court sense. He was a sharpshooter in the Larry Bird mold – strong enough that his range extended well beyond 20 feet – and also had a first step off the dribble to blow past defenders who came out to challenge his long-range bombs. Had the three-point arc been around earlier, Powell could have well advanced beyond his All-American career at Illinois State University.

"It was so long ago, I don't remember what he asked me in the first interview," said Powell, whose 90 points in four games led Joliet Central to third place in the '70 tournament. "But Don Ladas has always had that unique voice, and he's been instrumental in the sports world for many years.

"He's always been very positive and knowledgeable. When he talked to you, his words were very calming. He wasn't intimidating. He's aggressive, but he was passive with his aggression in terms of getting information out of a young kid."

Powell's son Roger Jr. also starred at Joliet. The younger Powell went on to play at the University of Illinois, helping the Illini to their first NCAA title game in school history. Roger Jr.'s 18 second-half points against Louisville lifted Illinois into the final and closed the circle on another memorable father-son Joliet sports parlay.

"They played different styles, but they were both great team players and both of them could really take over a game," Don said.

"Don Ladas is old school," said Powell the elder, an Illinois Youth Center employee who like Don has been a point man in numerous community functions. "He's from back in the blue collar era – unspoiled, and very appreciative of the opportunity he's had. He's never said anything derogatory. He knows how to word a delicate situation in a way that makes it flow. Don Ladas was, is, and always will be a legend in the sports world."

Roger Powell Jr. and Illinois came close in '05. North Carolina State did the full Cinderella number in 1983.

NC State won the NCAA basketball title that year with an amazing postseason run that was capped by a stunning two-point victory over heavily favored Houston in the championship game.

Houston was an explosive team led by future NBA Hall of Famers Hakeem Olajuwan and Clyde Drexler, and true to expectations, Hakeem the Dream and Clyde the Glide led the Cougars to an eight-point lead at halftime.

North Carolina State had no NBA-caliber superstars – just a bunch of guys who played great team ball throughout the playoffs and never quit.

They did have one of the best outside shooters in the country, though. Terry Gannon, a Joliet guy, led the nation in three-point shooting that year with 59 percent and holds the school record for career free throw percentage. Don first met him when his father, Jim Gannon, was the basketball coach at Joliet Catholic. Terry was a confirmed "gym rat" who shot buckets with the Catholic High players at practice, and at halftime of their games.

"I remember that well," said Gannon, who today travels the world covering sports for ABC/ESPN television. "I sat on the bench every game, went into the locker room every game, and every day after school my dad had one of his players pick me up and bring me to their practice. I first got to know Mr. Ladas through my dad."

North Carolina State took advantage of Houston's inability to hit free throws down the stretch and whittled away at the deficit, finally tying the game in the final half-minute. After a timeout, NC State had possession of the ball and a chance to win it with a final shot, so coach Jim Valvano, who pulled all the right strings throughout that postseason, put Gannon in the game.

It was a logical move, given both Gannon's accuracy from the perimeter and the fact that there was no one Valvano would have rather had shooting an important free throw.

Gannon didn't score in those final moments, but he made a big contribution. College basketball fans will remember Lorenzo Charles plucking a 30-foot airball by teammate Derrick Wittenburg and turning it into a game-winning dunk at the buzzer. The image of a euphoric Valvano running helter-skelter around the court afterward has been an NCAA highlight staple.

What most probably don't remember is that with 11 seconds to play Gannon deftly repelled a near steal. Drexler had knifed into a passing lane during the chaotic final moments and very nearly had the theft – which surely would have resulted in a breakaway slam at the other end – were it not for good positioning by Gannon to receive the pass near the free throw line. Two passes later, Wittenburg, forced far outside by Houston's pressure, hoisted up the shot that Charles would turn into one of the most replayed scenes in college-playoff history.

"Drexler was within an eyelash of taking it away," Gannon said. "Somehow I got my body in there to get in front of the ball and keep it from being a steal. The story behind that last possession was that after a time out, we had a plan, but Houston came out in a zone trap for the first time all game. It totally threw us all out of kilter. We were so disorganized; that's why the ball was all over the place. It was a miracle that we actually held on to it for that last shot. Guys were in positions they shouldn't have been in. It was supposed to be Sidney Lowe at the top of the key, penetrating as a point guard and dishing it to either Wittenburg on one side or me on the other side. I'm still wide open on that wing. On that final play, Witt, to this day, will tell you it was a pass.

"Mr. Ladas was a big part of it when we came back. They had ceremonies in Joliet to honor our national championship, and he helped with those. He's just been … he *is* Joliet sports. My recollections as a kid, of Catholic High basketball and my dad coaching – he's intertwined with that, calling all the games on the radio and being part of that. He was always a big figure to me."

Don was keeping score and calling the play-by-play when Gannon was an 11-year-old pitching and playing shortstop for the St. Joe's all-star baseball team. Gannon led that squad to back-to-back appearances in the championship game of the Boys Baseball World Series.

"I knew I'd reached the big time when Mr. Ladas was calling our games," he said. "I remember taping those games; I had somebody tape them on WJOL and I'd go back and listen to them. We lost in the championship game both times. Once it was to a team called Miami Cuba, although they were disqualified because they had some players who were too old. I think the catcher had a moustache. The other time we lost a 1-0 game to a team from California, a great game."

It wasn't the first time Don had covered a game where a Gannon was pitching. He was there when Jim Gannon recorded two punch-outs in one inning of a junior college baseball game.

Many pitchers routinely strike out the side, you say?

"Jim was pitching for Joliet," Don said, "and they were playing a team from LaGrange. There were twins on the

LaGrange team, and one of them got hit by a pitch. He must've thought it was intentional, because he charged the mound to fight. Jim knocked him down with one punch, so the twin brother rushed the mound, too, and Jim knocked *him* down with one punch. I never saw anything like that. Jim was a tough guy."

"He's told me that on the air before," Terry Gannon said, laughing. "You know what? It's in character. I totally believe that."

As it has been observed, loyalty to a sports team can be factored down to cheering for uniforms, for laundry. The reviled nemesis from an opposing team is suddenly looked at in a different light when he's traded to yours. A.J. Pierczinski was a dirty-playing catcher before he became a take-charge winner with the White Sox. Bulls fans didn't mind that Dennis Rodman came to town with a little baggage, as long as he grabbed his 18 rebounds every game.

That idea that uniforms are secondary to the guys wearing them was well-demonstrated during Don's recruiting of major-league players to participate in the MS Benefit softball games. Dyed-in-the-wool White Sox fan Don found his warmest reception and most success locking in big-league players on the North Side corner of Clark and Addison.

That's right. It was a bunch of good-hearted Cubs players in the mid-'70s who made the MS Benefit a huge success.

"I don't think you could do it today," Don said. "But back then I went into the locker room and asked a few of the guys if they were interested – Jose Cardenal, Manny Trillo and George

Mitterwald all said yes, and then some of the other players heard us talking and said, 'Can I come too?' It was great. They were such good guys. Like I said, this was 30 years ago and I don't think you could go in there cold and get a lot of players to agree to do something like that."

Mitterwald, a career .236 hitter, blasted three home runs in one game at Rivals Park.

"He asked if he could play the rest of his games in Joliet," Don said.

But what happened with Trillo was even better. The Cubs players joined Don and some others after another benefit game, and Trillo was the life of the party, staying until closing time, long after his teammates had gone.

"We had a great time," Don said. "By the end of the night Manny was up there playing a trombone and singing. It was one of the most fun times we had at the MS game."

But Trillo, an all-star second baseman, was sleeping off some of the fun and missed the Cubs' flight to San Francisco the next day. He took a private plane, but arrived late. When he was inserted into the game, he committed an error that opened the door to a one-run Giants victory.

"He told me about it the next year," Don said. "He said, 'It was your fault! Because of that night, we lost!'"

Don, who couldn't stifle the Sox voice within, said, "Well, Manny, nice going. Thanks!"

Before the proliferation of media that came with cable television and the Internet, Don had a job with NBC radio doing updates and wrap-ups from Comiskey Park and Wrigley Field.

"I'd go on every three innings and say something like, 'The Sox took a 5-3 lead on Jorge Orta's fourth home run of the year, and after loading the bases with no outs, Rich Gossage worked out of the jam and that's where we are now.' Postgame stuff, too. I had a good time doing that, and I met a lot of nice guys."

One of them was Don Buford of the White Sox, who persuaded Don to let him take the microphone once and do an interview with one of his teammates.

"He did a good job with it," Don said. "It worked out well."

Don was a radio journalist, and also a fan. He brought a 16-inch softball to the 1983 all-star game at Comiskey Park and got autographs. And just as he'd been star-struck in his first interview with a big name – quarterback Otto Graham, at the College All-Star Game – he still got nervous around the stars.

"I'd be talking to Willie Mays or someone like that and I'd think, 'What are these guys doing talking to *me*? I just loved being in there. I couldn't imagine a better job," he said.

Not all of the players were friendly – he recalls the Dodgers' Wes Parker looking condescendingly and asking, "What the hell do you want?" – but most of them were helpful and receptive. When Ron Blomberg came to the White Sox in 1978, he told Don about the fight he'd seen between Bill Sudakis and Rick Dempsey when they were breaking in together with the Yankees.

"I guess it was a real John Wayne-Ward Bond blowout," Don said. "They were rolling down the stairs and really going after each other. The Yankees front office heard about it and released both of them the next day."

Sudakis went to the Dodgers, where as a promising rookie he was pictured with Ron Cey and Steve Garvey in a 1969 Sports Illustrated cover.

Don shot pool with Sudakis, a Joliet native, at a bar in Rockdale called Shep's.

"Billy got so mad when he missed a shot once he raised his cue stick over his head and accidentally broke a lamp on top of the table," Don said. "All Shep said was, 'Thirty-nine dollars.' Billy paid him and we wiped off the table and finished the game in the dark. I think I won that game. To beat Billy Sudakis at anything was good. He's such a competitor. Good bowler, too. He got on PBA Bowling Tour for a while. I told him, 'You're not good enough to be on the Tour!' He said, 'Well, I'm on it.'

"He wore contact lenses, but once he had them in the wrong eyes. And during that time, he went on his longest hitting streak. He changed the contacts, but later I asked him why he didn't leave them in the wrong way. He said, 'Hey, I never thought of that.' "

Insomniacs today can battle their problem with a portable "sound soother" machine that mimics various sounds designed to help produce a soft background noise conducive to deeper Z's. The sleep-deprived can choose from a number of settings, including the metronomic drone of a heartbeat; the hypnotic blasting of ocean waves at high tide and a mesmerizing chorus of crickets and wind swirling through the summer night.

For Don's daughter Sheri, the comforting background noise that put her to sleep as a young girl was the clicking of a typewriter.

"We were at the house on Caroline Drive where my parents moved in 1970, when they were expecting me," Sheri said. "It was a ranch house where my mom's parents remodeled our two-car attached garage into a recreation room that we called 'the other room.' I don't know why, but that's what we called it. 'Where's Dad?' 'He's working out in the other room.' The other room was where we kept our toys, an exercise bicycle, a cedar closet, a bar area, a trophy case and a pool table from the old Chalk and Cue.

"It was also his office, which was always piled high with papers color-coded by bowling alley for the scores he'd be announcing. There was a hard-wired phone and a desk with a small area cleared out and reserved for his Underwood typewriter. It wasn't one of the fancy electric ones that my mom used, but an old-fashioned manual one with ribbon. That's the typewriter I learned on when I was old enough to start learning how to spell. I remember wanting to sit in front of that typewriter and emulate him. And I remember falling asleep to the tune of that typewriter. You could hear through the air vents in my room the clanks of the keys, the bells and the return motions. It all had a rhythm to it. I remember laying there and listening almost like it was music.

"Isn't that a weird thing to remember? But I can still hear those sounds now, in my mind. I used to count the key strokes to see how high I could count up to. I don't think I ever told him that, but it was like a game. When we moved to the next home, I couldn't hear the typewriter any more and for months

I had a hard time falling asleep, not knowing he was close by, typing away into the wee hours of the night."

Don isn't exactly riding the edge of modern electronic technology. He still uses the manual typewriter. He doesn't have a computer, or any sort of access to e-mail.

"In this day of radio, with the way the budget is, you have to be able to do everything," Don's friend and co-worker Scott Slocum said. "To this day, Don still can't plug a microphone into a mixer. He always told me, 'I never wanted to get involved in that, so I never learned it.'

"That goes back to the respect thing. He's earned so much respect that nobody's ever told him, 'Learn this, or you're gone.' If you've survived as many station owners as Don has survived, it means one thing and one thing only – that you have an ability to make money for the radio station, and the way you make money is by being popular and respected, and he's both of those."

The bottom line is, of course, the bottom line. And Don still puts up prolific sales numbers.

"For our baseball tournament," Slocum said, "he just went out and sold 30 sponsors. Thirty! The rest of the sales staff sold eight, combined. Most sales people come up with these fancy, glossy sales pitches. Don will say, 'Hey, we've got this going on. I know you've supported it in the past. I imagine you'll want to support it again?' How do you say no to that? How do you say no to a legend?"

Slocum will probably inherit the responsibility of maintaining many of Don's accounts in the event he decides to retire.

"The general manager has talked to me about taking over that spot. I've been around here long enough where I can kind of do the same thing and make calls like that. But it's not going to be the same. You don't say no to Don."

Angie was ambivalent, at best, about the spring-training vacations that the Ladases took every year.

"I didn't enjoy spring training," the 35-year-old mother of two said. "It was great that we got to go on vacation, but when we were out on the field watching the games I'd be thinking, 'When do we get to go swimming?' I had no desire to watch ballgames, to go to the ballpark and sit there. It was hot. This is going to sound terrible, but I'm so not a fan. I think it's because I was so used to … it was on TV at home all the time. When my dad was home he'd always watch sports. That's all that was on. I think I'm numb to it."

But like every self-respecting kid seeking a favorable result, Angie also knew that the sports-on-TV street ran both ways.

"If you ever wanted something from him, you'd ask while he was watching a game," she said. "It would always be, 'Yeah, sure, fine.' If he was watching a game that he was really interested in I don't think he'd hear a bomb go off. He was stuck in his own little world."

Don Jr. wasn't bothered by the sports overload. He liked baseball. Like his old man, he was a good player. His dad helped arrange for him to be a batboy at a White Sox game in 1984.

"I still have the broken bat that Greg Luzinski gave me after that game," Don Jr. said. "He hit a double with it, and gave it to me. It was a great day doing that. I got to meet a lot of pro athletes because of the work my dad is in. I remember meeting Bo Jackson. That was pretty cool. My dad would always bring me signed baseballs, new baseball gloves and stuff like that. He was gone a lot on weekends, but when he was home I'd always play catch with him or basketball in the driveway. When he was home he'd always make up for the time he was gone."

Angie could have taken or left the spring training games. Her sister loved them.

"I couldn't get enough," Sheri said. "Payne Park was one of my earliest memories. I used to love hanging out at the ballpark. I think I remember reading that the White Sox trained there for 44 years. I'll bet my dad was a huge part of that legacy.

"I loved going to all the games he covered. He'd let me hang the WJOL banner, and sometimes I got to sit with the extra set of earphones on so I could hear the broadcast. I remember going to Pony League opening days and all of the local high school and college games. I was with him at Lewis when he celebrated his 100th broadcast of the basketball game there. I have so many memories of sitting with him at booths, in the area where he was a fixture, and then being older and going to games socially and seeing him there in his 'Spot.' I was so proud of him and I always will be."

The nature of Don's breathless work schedule may have rendered him an absentee dad on weekends, but, as Angie noted, he never missed the big stuff.

"For anything important, he was always there," she said. "I don't remember being mad, or resenting him for being gone. When I was little, really little, I remember him coming home from work. It was the greatest moment of my day. He always made it very special when he came home from work, always made it a point to talk to us, to hug us and let us know he was home. He always made the most of it when he was home."

And he let his actions set the model his kids grew up with.

"His best trait is his persistence," Angie said. "He's seventy-some years old and he still goes to work every day. He's a very honorable man. He doesn't ever give up. He taught us to never give up. He's probably one of the most amazing people I know."

Don. Jr. played basketball and football in high school until a bout with mononucleosis in his sophomore year forced him to miss the basketball season. From that point, his sports career at Joliet Catholic was focused on football.

Angie and Sheri didn't play sports in high school but both cheered on the Joliet Catholic Academy poms squad that won a national championship in a competition televised on ESPN.

"So I can tease Donnie and Jonathan that we made it on national TV and they didn't," Sheri said.

Sheri started dating Jonathan Voss in 1985, when they were sophomores in high school. Voss, a natural leader, was a three-sport athlete who played quarterback, point guard and catcher at Joliet Catholic.

"I'd met Don Ladas before, when I was palling around with my dad (Bob) at Lockport High School," Voss said. "But I didn't put two and two together until Sheri and I started dating."

Bob Voss was an assistant football coach at Lockport before taking a job to work on Gordie Gillespie's staff at St. Francis.

"My dad couldn't be at a lot of games that I played in because he was coaching at St. Francis," Jonathan said. "Not that Don would ever take the place of my dad, but in a lot of respects Don was like a second father to me. So instead of my dad getting my slanted point of view on what happened in the game, Don would be on the radio telling my dad exactly what did happen. It obviously made for a lot of fun."

The ultimate fun for Voss at Joliet Catholic came in November of '87. The Hilltoppers lost two games in the regular season but came together in the playoffs under second-year coach Jim Boyter. They rallied from 13 points down in the second half to win by one point, with Voss throwing the deciding touchdown pass in the final two minutes.

"It was a great win, and Don spoke with a bunch of us afterward, as usual," Voss said. "But my most vivid memory of talking with him on the air during those playoffs was the semifinal against Belvidere."

On one of the coldest and windiest days of the year, Joliet Catholic advanced to the title game by knocking off host Belvidere, a school which at the time didn't have the most accommodating press box. With no room inside for WJOL to set up shop, Don and Scott were left to do the game al fresco.

"They announced the game from the top of the school," Voss said. "They interviewed me afterward, and they had to lower the microphone down from a long cord. I was on the ground looking up and getting interviewed from the top of a building, with the microphone blowing back and forth in the wind."

Jonathan and Sheri stayed together, and a strong friendship grew between Don and Mary Lou and Bob and Chris Voss.

"The biggest thing has always been the closeness of our families," Jonathan said. "Whether it's the Ladases or the Vosses. All four parents are so humble. There are no hidden agendas."

Their uninterrupted state of comity has even survived the most harrowing of litmus tests.

"He'll always find a way to throw a jab at me about being a Cubs fan," Voss said. "I hope I haven't punished my kids by making them Cubs fans; they're going to have to deal with all that futility all their lives.

"The thing for me growing up around Don was how easy everything was, how uncomplicated everything was. Everything always seemed to flow. It was always a good, enjoyable time. I remember asking him for permission to marry Sheri, and being absolutely petrified, just coming to this man who I have so much respect for and asking him that type of question, wondering if he's going to say no. I think he started laughing at me, but he didn't make it harder on me than it already was. He probably saw my sweaty armpits and realized how nervous I was."

If Jonathan has been an ideal son-in-law to Don and Mary Lou, the reverse is also true.

"What you see is what you get with Don and Mary Lou," Jonathan said. "I've never had to work hard to try and impress them. They've made it so easy on Sheri and me as a couple because we literally grew up together, and we saw with our four parents such good examples of how parents should be."

Once during the 1988 state baseball finals Don turned over the microphone to Jonathan, as he had done with Don Buford when he covered the White Sox. Buford made good use of his chance as an interviewer, and so did the future son-in-law. He interviewed teammate Chris Michalak, an outstanding left-handed pitcher who would go on to play major league ball with Arizona, Toronto, Texas and Cincinnati.

"I was a little leery of appearing to favor Jonathan because he was my daughter's boyfriend," Don said. "But he deserved to be there. He was the quarterback and the catcher and the point guard. He was a leader on those teams. Heck, I probably gave him more of the spotlight than I gave my own son."

Don Ladas Jr. had grown to 6-foot-5 and 235 pounds by his senior year. He was an all-area offensive tackle and helped Joliet Catholic establish one of the most effective running attacks in the state.

For Don Sr., announcing Joliet Catholic football games presented a pleasant quandary. There was on the one hand the enormous welling of pride in watching his son perform at a high level on a team with a chance to go far in the state playoffs.

But he was also mindful of never overdoing it. Just as Hall of Fame quarterback-turned-announcer Bob Griese faced a challenge in appearing neutral when he did his son Brian's games on ABC, Don was judicious in dishing out the superlatives to describe Joliet Catholic's offensive right tackle.

"He interviewed the whole offensive line one time," Don Jr. said. "He always said he wanted to do one of my games. He said he'd retire after he did one of them. He said that a couple of times."

There were inside scoops that Don was privy to while his boy was playing on the team. Some of the stuff might have made interesting filler during timeouts or first-down measurements.

He could have, for instance, shared with WJOL listeners the story about how the offensive lineman and star running back took a car that wasn't theirs to cruise over to some girls' houses late at night during the week.

"I took his car out a lot of times," Don Jr. said. "But I always tried to get it back before he and my mom got home, or if they were home, to have it back without them noticing. But one night Mike and I were out visiting some girls and when I pulled into the driveway, my mom and dad were both standing there. It wasn't a late night, but I guess it was late enough. I got grounded for that one."

Don Jr. and Mike Alstott were best of friends since second grade, and grew even closer during their junior and senior years, when Alstott was making a name for himself.

Alstott combined a bear-like strength with surprising speed, deftness and a low center of gravity to emerge as one of the premier running backs in Illinois. He led coach Bob Stone's Joliet Catholic team to the 1990 Class 4A state championship.

"We ran the ball about every down – I think we passed about three times a game," said Alstott, who went on to become an All-American fullback at Purdue and an All-Pro with the Tampa Bay Buccaneers. Alstott's piledriving style and hard-nosed work ethic would make him a favorite of football announcers throughout the NFL, and the most popular player in the franchise's history.

"Donnie was one of my best friends, and we dominated together," he said. "I got to grow up around Don Sr. because I was friends with Don Jr.,"

In thundering his way to an All-American career at Purdue, Alstott made fools of college scouts who'd determined that he wouldn't cut it as a big-time running back. He did likewise to the pro scouts who still hadn't learned. Alstott, who was passed over in the 1996 draft until Tampa took him in the second round, went to six straight Pro Bowls.

"And he worked for everything he got," Don said. "That's one great kid, and one great football player. Yes, you could see when he was in high school that he was going on to big things. He had a lot of ability, but what set him apart from a lot of the others was the way he worked. He was a good player and he made himself a great player."

For a sports fan/athlete like Alstott growing up in Joliet, kind words from Don Ladas Sr. were praise from Caesar.

"Don is the voice of Joliet and always will be," Alstott said. "There's no question that he's someone we looked up to as a professional person, a celebrity, a voice of reason and also a father figure. Being around his house all the time, it was easy to see how he inspired young people. He inspired people of all ages in Joliet, with his positive attitude and the things he's said. Talk about a nice guy. There's not a mean bone in his body."

Teenagers may not demonstrate the best judgment at all times, but they have a better handle on detecting breeches in integrity than many adults would like to believe.

"What you see is what you get with Don Ladas," Alstott said. "He didn't change from he who was in his professional life to who he was when he got home. He was always the same person. That's something you really admire. You look at all the things he's done to keep everyone abreast of what's going on, and how he's worked to keep Joliet a close-knit sports community, and for how long he's done it. It's really something. He's someone I'll remember for a long time and look back on and say he was a big part of my life."

With respect to the nebulous web of sports history in Joliet, there are no six degrees of separation. There is one degree of separation, and it is Don Ladas. Don has covered the star players of the era, and years later covered their kids, and then their grandkids. He's interviews coaches who he used to interview as players. And sometimes he's right there in the booth working alongside the guys he used to cover when they were playing and coaching.

Mack McLaughlin had been a defensive back and punt returner with the Saskatchewan Roughriders of the Canadian Football League before he came to Joliet in 1965. He played for Joliet's semipro Chargers football team before settling into a successful career teaching and coaching wrestling (43 years), softball (23 years) and football (21 years).

"Don was always there for me," Mack said. "At first, after every Chargers game he'd come up and try to talk to me and I was too shy to say much of anything to him. But once we got to know each other, it was great communicating with him. We had some great times with the trips we went on."

McLaughlin recalls the trip Don made with the Chargers to a game in Minnesota, after which someone broke out a deck of cards and a whole new game began.

"I don't think I made much money playing with them," McLaughlin said. "But Don had a good time. He's quite a character with a few beers in him. He can sing a lot of songs and tell a lot of stories when he gets wound up. Don was always funny when we had those card games. It was a pleasure to be around those guys."

Not surprisingly, McLaughlin appreciates Don's diplomatic touch reporting on young athletes, and what he's come to mean to him as a friend.

"He's just a great gentleman," he said. "And he has a work ethic. That encouraged me a lot. I've had four back surgeries and knee-replacement surgery, and after all these surgeries people would ask me if I could do things like walk up stairs. I thought, if Don Ladas can walk up the steps, I can walk up the steps. I drew courage from him. I'd see him limping along with his briefcase and no hat on, walking around, walking up the steps, and that helped give me the will to keep going on and being effective."

McLaughlin has expanded his métier and today keeps going on and being effective as a radio and cable TV sports announcer.

"I picked up a lot of anecdotes and other things I use as an announcer from listening to him," he said. "The big thing I learned from him is that you tell it like it is. You relate what happens on the field in a way that's educational, and you never put a kid down. A kid who's out there busting his butt should be encouraged no matter how he's performing. Don has always done that. People would be fascinated by the things he knows. He has a great insight for sports."

Mark Mulder won 21 games with the Oakland A's to lead the American League in 2001, and also led the league twice in shutouts and complete games. The left-handed pitcher established himself as one of the game's best in 2003 and '04, and was named to the American League All-Star team in those two seasons.

But in the semifinal of the 1994 Class 2A state tournament Mulder was unable to hold a 6-5 lead in the last inning of South Holland Thornwood's game against Joliet Catholic. Mulder had been summoned to protect the lead after Thornwood scored five unearned runs against coach Joe Rodeghero's Hilltoppers. Joliet Catholic, which committed seven errors in that game – after playing errorless ball in all six of the playoff games before it – managed to nick Mulder for a run in the seventh to send it into extra innings, and then won it 7-6 with a run in the eighth.

Rodeghero is another local athlete and coach who has done the Ladas full circle. He was first interviewed by Don in 1970, when Rodeghero played on the Joliet Colt League team that finished third at the World Series in Lafayette, Indiana.

"That was my first time being interviewed by anyone," he said. "Don was there doing the game, by himself, I imagine. I was shocked that I was on the radio because of who he was.

Everyone knew who he was. Growing up in the area, WJOL and Don Ladas are the same word. If anyone says WJOL is here, you look to see where Don Ladas is. He's the icon around here, and there will never be anyone like him because of his longevity."

Rodeghero completed the Don Ladas cycle when he put on the headset to announce his first basketball game.

"During a break, or before the game, I said something to him about that," Rodeghero said. "I reminded him of how he interviewed me when I was 16, and then of how he was the first one to interview me when I was a coach. When he does a game, he'll talk about how this kid's father played for Gordie, or how Don played with the kid's grandfather. I've never heard him say one negative thing about anyone. He can tell a lot of stories off the cuff, and he remembers everything. To me, that's what's most impressive about him."

Of course, the competitor-turned-boothmate sequence wouldn't be complete without a bowler.

George Kontos of Joliet was a member of the team that survived a field of 17,000 to win the 2001 American Bowling Congress' national tournament. Don was immediately burning up the phone lines preparing the festivities.

He organized a banquet to commemorate the feat, dredging up memorabilia from both the Joliet-area team that won the event in 1976, and the Hub Recreational squad that claimed the title back in the 1920s.

"Don had a huge hand in the increase in bowling popularity and growth in the area," Kontos said. "The Chicagoland area is a pretty strong bowling community, but the Joliet area is especially strong, considering the number of households we draw from. Don played a big part in spreading the word. Not many areas have what he's brought to our area. He's bridged a lot of gaps, made a lot of believers. I think a lot of bowlers might not have got involved, or stayed involved in bowling, if it wasn't for the credibility he brought to it with his broadcasts. A lot of players today grew up with their parents having listened to him on the radio."

Don and Kontos have teamed up to do a cable TV presentation of the Will County Open tournament for the past 10 years.

"It's amazing how much I can learn just sitting next to him," Kontos said. "It's cool for me; there's a good chemistry with Don. He likes to tell a lot of stories from the past. Everybody likes it. Everybody talks about it.

"I've been around Don a lot and I've never heard him say a bad word about anybody. No matter who you bring up, he's got a story to tell about him or her. If it's not about bowling, it's about when he played baseball with him as a kid, or when he was broadcasting Belmont Little League games. Bowling has been a big part of it, but his career is a lot more in-depth than just bowling. He was an athlete, too. He played softball seriously until he was about 60."

Don's eternally optimistic message is not to be confused with how he understands the cold realities of the real world. He understands that economics drive small businesses and corporations alike, and that arguing money can be a volatile endeavor.

He almost fought with a bar owner during a sales pitch when the owner stopped him in mid-spiel and cursed him and his technique.

"I didn't go there to get insulted," Don said. "If you don't want to buy air time, don't buy it. But I don't have to listen to someone bad-mouth me. Luckily I had a few friends at the bar who intervened, so nothing happened. And I don't know how I'd have done against him, but he would've known he was in a fight."

"Over the years, the radio station has changed owners," Matt Senffner said. "And he had to argue with corporate about keeping high school sports on the air. Most guys go to work and say, 'OK, what do I have to do?' And that's it, and they get pushed around by corporate. I really admire a guy who argues with corporate and sticks with what he believes. Don has had to hustle a lot of money to make it cost-effective to keep sports on the radio. I honestly believe that without him, and guys like Don Hazen and Bob Drazkowski, high school sports would not be in the limelight in our area like they are.

"Especially so with Don Ladas. He pushed to get the games on FM (WJTW, WJOL's sister station), which was big because they broadcast the FM games on Saturdays and that's when we played. It was exciting in the early days to get a game on the radio."

The early days at Providence Catholic High School included Senffner coaching a bunch of underclass football players, and young Providence still working out the details of its athletic infrastructure.

"I remember Don and Frank O'Leary doing games out here when we had a homemade press box sitting on top of a couple of telephone polls," Senffner said. "He and Frank climbed a ladder to get in there. Sometimes, if there were too many people in the box, they have to go out and sit on top, outside. But Don never complained about it. He was always prepared."

By the time he retired as Providence football coach in 2005, Senffner had helped turn Providence into a program that won six state championships, including a run of three straight during a stretch that encompassed 50 consecutive victories.

"He'll never criticize a coach or berate a player," Senffner said. "It's always, 'Everybody's working hard out there, doing a whale of a job.' The other thing about him is, if you want to know something, he's the guy to ask. He'll say, 'Remember this game, Matt?' I'd say not really. I've coached about 300 games. But he's done about 3,300 games and he still remembers so many of them so vividly. One of the biggest honors I've had is to present him to the Joliet Area Hall of Fame."

Don has a ready explanation of how he came to be inducted in the Illinois Sportscasters Hall of Fame, the Illinois Basketball Hall of Fame, the Illinois State Bowling Hall of Fame, the Joliet Junior College Hall of Fame, the Joliet/Will County Hall of Pride, the Will County Bowling Hall of Fame and the Minor League/Pro Football National Hall of Fame – which is the same explanation for why he was named University of St. Francis Man of the Year and Unico Man of the Year.

"They had to give it to someone and they couldn't find anyone else," Don says. "I was probably the last one left."

Whatever you say, Don.

He's not the only one in the house to have been honored. Mary Lou recently won the Mary Frances Veeck Woman of the Year Award.

"That award is for basically understanding that your husband is away most of the time," said Mary Lou, who was also honored later by the Hit and Pitch Club of Chicago. "I was very humbled by the award, very excited. My co-workers surprised me by buying a table and coming up to be there. That's what made it fun. But I'm not a limelight person. Don is the limelight guy and I'm more background.

"When he's won those awards, it was a source of pride for me, too. I see how much work he puts into things. He never does anything halfway, he just gives it his all. And he's a very loyal person. If a gas station is a sponsor, he'll support them. If he makes a commitment, you better believe he's going to carry it through. That breed is almost gone."

If he had his way, Don would extend the limelight to everyone in the area code. Don is on the nominating committee for the Joliet Area Sports Hall of Fame, whose other members include Joliet Herald News sports editor Dick Goss.

"From a logistical standpoint, we have to limit the number of inductees to six or eight a year," Goss said. "From a Ladas perspective, we should be inducting 500 every year. He has a mile-long list that he brings to the meetings. Others might argue that some on the list may not be worthy of a Hall of Fame of this magnitude, but not Don. They are all Hall of Famers in his book."

Goss grew up in Joliet, and after going away to college he returned to take the sports editor position at the Herald News in 1983.

"From the time I was a little kid listening to basketball and football games on the radio – and to all the summer baseball games – I would get out my transistor radio, put it under my pillow and listen to Don Ladas's call," he said. "It's impossible to have been in this area anytime since the 1950s and to not recognize his voice. So many of the athletes and coaches he's covered have become his friend. The thing about him is, he loves people.

"I've never known a more genuine, caring person than him. In a business where print and electronic media sometimes try to one-up each other, Don and I have always helped each other out. He's a legend, all right. But his humility and his caring for the people of Joliet through the years make him what he is."

Dan Sharp gets a kick out of Don's cracker-jack style of calling a game.

"He always had a very colorful way of doing it," Sharp said. "He kept in interesting, using terms like 'stanzas' and 'gosh-darnit,' and 'doing a whale of a job.' What I remember most about Don is he always found the positive side about the athletes and coaches."

Gordie Gillespie said Don is the type of guy he'd hire as an assistant coach, the kind of guy who would dig down in the trenches, doing all the dirty jobs and doing them well.

Sharp was one of those assistant football coaches, digging down in the trenches coach at Joliet Catholic, before assuming the reins. He's worked out OK as a head coach. In November of '07, Sharp, a classy leader in the Gillespie mold, won his sixth state championship at the school.

"Don has given his support through all of them, as usual," Sharp said. "It's always been a joy to listen to him because you got a flavor of not only what was going on in the game, but also the feeling about the families and the kids and the people. You got to know them from his broadcasts.

"The other thing I found out about him is how charitable he is and how many things he's done. He started a scholarship fund on his own, and he does so many fundraisers. It amazed me how much he means to the Joliet community, and how lucky the Joliet community is to have a guy like him living here. He's made so many friends, and he's so kind to everybody. A kind person can be popular."

There are no dress rehearsals for parenthood. The curtain goes up, and you're on – break a leg!

Grandchildren are nature's mulligan. Something you didn't like about the way you did it the last time? Go ahead, tee it up again.

"As a grandparent, oh my God … I don't want to say my dad's even better as a grandfather than as a father," Angie said, "but he's fantastic."

Don's first grandchild came from his second daughter. Angie's son Trent, who is now 13, lived with Don and Mary Lou until he was five.

Angie and her husband Pete Kapellas, an automobile wholesaler, also have one-year-old Tessa. Jonathan and Sheri Voss have 11-year-old Drew, six-year-old Abigail and four-year-old Aidan.

Because of their time spent together in the formative years, there will always be a certain connection between Trent and his grandparents.

"My dad taught him how to count by using playing cards, when Trent was two years old," Angie said. "He also taught him how to count money, which is why Trent to this day is obsessed with money. My dad loves all his grandkids the same, but there's a special bond with Trent because he lived with him for so long."

To the surprise of no one who knows him, Don is visibly moved when the topic of his grandkids is raised.

"They're all just so very special to me and Mary Lou," he said. "They bring us a lot of happiness."

Drew is a three-sport guy, like his dad, and has enjoyed the taste of victory as a football, basketball and baseball player.

"He's the kind of kid who could be a good varsity athlete," Jonathan says of his son. "He'll outwork a lot of guys."

Drew sees only one fault in his grandfather.

"There's just one bad thing," he said. "He's a Sox fan. I always make jokes about the Sox and he does the same with the Cubs. My papa has always been cheerful. I don't think he even has a temper. He's always been there for me. I remember playing ball with him out in the backyard when I was real little – that always made me happy. My mom is lucky she has him as a dad. I will always love him."

Don was in the booth calling the play-by-play in the sixth inning of a tie game at the championship of the WJOL-sponsored baseball tournament when Slocum asked to borrow the headset of Steve Brandy, who was doing the game with Don.

"Mary Lou had called me on my cell," Slocum said. "I interrupted for a second and said, 'Don, there's something very important I have to tell you.' He turned around kind of slowly and said, 'What is it?' I said, 'Well, as of a few moments ago, we now have a third Don Ladas on the planet.'"

Don Jr., a construction worker, and his wife Sarah (nee Kozak, a middle hitter for coach Julie Hudson's 1993 Lockport High School state champion volleyball team) had just given Don his sixth grandchild.

"When I said those words, he whipped around like he was 25 years old," Slocum said. "I said, 'Your son Donnie and Sarah just gave birth to a 7-pound, 12-ounce baby boy named Don Ladas III.' He literally broke down on the air and sobbed."

Throw fastballs for 20 years and eventually your shoulder starts to fray. Cover games every weekend after doing your daily radio show and making your daily sales rounds and doing all the charity events and community functions, and eventually the needle of the tank creeps toward E.

Don endured what may have been a bout with exhaustion in the summer of 1993, when he woke up in the middle of the night unable to breath. It felt like he was being strangled.

"It was just out of the blue," he said. "I just woke up choking. I thought I was gone."

Mary Lou called the hospital, which ran a battery of tests that revealed nothing.

So Don went right back to work and covered a softball game, but the wind-blown dirt from the infield made it almost impossible for him to breathe again. Back to the hospital he went.

And back out, with no firm diagnosis. That weekend he went to the wedding of Suzanne Fitzgerald, the daughter of Tom Fitzgerald, Don's brother-in-law.

"There was no way I was going to miss that," Don said. "The whole ordeal with the choking really put a different perspective on my life. It really humbled me. I know we're all going to go sometime, but when I was lying there in bed gasping for breath, all I could think of was, 'Not yet! Not yet!'

"I can remember walking out the door to cover a game or go to a banquet, while my daughter would be in her prom dress. Things like that, when I should've been around but couldn't because of work, I see now that those are the moments that mean everything."

Panic is understandable when you can't breathe. When the specter of mortality gets up in your face, your outlook tends to change. He needn't have worried about missed opportunities with his family, though, because as the kids all point out, quality trumps quantity. Don was always there when it mattered.

He's in no rush to leave this earth, so he decided to pull back a little. He swore off the long hours and the cold calls and the banquets – a bold resolution for a perpetual-motion machine like him.

The new, laid-back pace lasted about 45 minutes. It's not easy to instantly change the nature of whom and what you are. He pressed the pedal back to the floor and kept it there, covering more games and appearing at more functions, always in motion, always in the middle of the action.

But then came the back pain in early 2007. And the headaches, the constant, pounding headaches. Neither ailment sorted itself out, and after a few months of chronic discomfort and pain, Don checked into Mayo Clinic in the fall.

"We've been trying to convince him to slow down, to go part-time, to give up something," Sheri said. "But for my dad, working at WJOL isn't what he does. It's who he is. And ending that part about who he has been for the past 54 years is not an easy matter. His retirement won't be easy, even if it's a well-planned process. Someone asked me not long ago what his hobbies are. He really has no hobbies. He loves what he does and it completes him. He knows nothing else and still needs all the pieces to feel whole."

"I've seen him go full circle," Slocum said. "From a tough guy who will scratch and claw with anybody, to a guy who has realized what life has given him. I think he's appreciating it. For all these years, he's worked and worked and worked. I've said to him, 'Why don't you retire?' He said, 'Scott, if I retire, I'm gonna die.' But I think he realizes now that he's had a great life, and maybe he doesn't need to work as hard anymore."

"Some days he wants to retire," Don Jr. said, "but he's miserable at home. He can't stand still. I think he's just going to do it until … until that's it. It's his life, you know? It's what he does, it's what he wants to do and he enjoys it. I don't know too many people who can say they really enjoy going to work. But he does. And he's the greatest dad in the world."

Don got roasted on a beautiful Friday Joliet night in October of '07. Friday in the autumn may be the worst possible time to hold a sports-related banquet because everyone is at a football game.

But that's when the banquet hall was available, and that's when people came out and filled the place anyway, paying tribute to the guy who has been such a big part of their lives.

Pat Sullivan was there, and so was Irish O'Reilly, the retired baseball coach at Lewis University.

"He's one of the good guys," said O'Reilly, a member of the American Baseball Coaches Association Hall of Fame. "Don is a good man, a good Christian, and he's done so much for sports in our area. He's contributed a lot to the advancement of athletics in our area, and the nice thing is, he's continued to do it. He's like Gordie Gillespie – he keeps ticking.

"I remember I was about 14 years old playing Pony League baseball in Kankakee. We beat a team from Joliet, which was almost unthinkable because they were unstoppable at the time. Don remembered that game almost pitch-by-pitch, which was fantastic, I thought. It was good to be at his roast because it's nice to recognize people when they're still alive. A lot of times, honors come after the fact. Don has never looked for any honors. He's just always been there, plugging away trying to get more sports on the radio. He's helped our university a lot, and the whole Joliet area, for sure."

The Vosses were there, as were Don's kids and their spouses. Don's old buddy Jim Ward was on hand, as were Earl D'Amico, Chuck Harris, Larry Bernard, Dennis Duffels, Jim Hall and Kent Irvin. Hall coached the Lockport baseball team that won one of the five high school state championships that the school garnered during Irvin's reign as athletic director.

The Voice Of Joliet

Don's old WJOL colleagues were there, too. Frank O'Leary, Bill Drilling and Ralph Sherman all went to the podium and took their good-natured shots at the venerated roastee.

But Don wasn't moving too well that night. Apart from the trip to Mayo, he'd been in and out of hospitals for the past two months. As it was 15 years earlier when Don woke up in the middle of the night unable to breathe, the diagnoses were inconclusive.

"He hates the fact that he's getting old," Mary Lou said. "He still wants to run five miles every day and play racquetball."

Two months from his 79th birthday, moving gingerly and surrounded by many friends who had already hung up their work boots and called it a career, Don was still reluctant to hang up the WJOL headset.

Sheri wasn't surprised. She'd grasped the extent of her father's loyalty to the radio station the day she told him she was leaving her job at AT&T.

"I'd been there eight years," she said. "Nowadays, working eight years at one place is a long time. But I remember him looking at me like, 'But you haven't given back what they've given you.' He's always fair. And I've never heard him say a bad word."

He may have uttered a few under his breath when the doctors at Mayo suggested he consider retiring.

Fifty-four years – where did they go? It didn't seem that long ago to Don that he and Frank and Mary Lou and the gang were going out after work, owning the day with youthful abandon. The whole WJOL ride has been a joy for Don, which is what makes giving it up so hard.

A light snow is falling from the February morning sky and Don is sitting alone at a table waiting to meet a friend at a donut shop, his face pained from the headaches and the weight of a decision. Customers pour in and out and Don recognizes a few faces, exchanging his usual pleasantries.

Joined at the table by his friend, Don reflected on his radio career, his health at 79 years old and the nagging prospect of retirement.

Endings of every sort are at least mildly depressing. Graduations, breakups, even closing time on a good night at a bar – they all serve as subconscious reminders that everything is temporary, and that ultimately we are all just passin' through.

"Retirement, that's what bothers me," Don says. "You do what makes you happy. I've been doing this for 54 years. I think it's time … I do what I want to do. I don't think I should."

He has no problem giving up the sales calls, or the Will County Sportsman newspaper. And after climbing press box stairs for more than half a century he might even be fine leaving that to someone else, too.

But there is one thing about his job he doesn't want to let go.

"Ten Pin Topics," he said. "I know it's not about me and it's probably no big deal, but if I quit, it's gone. I hate to let the bowlers down. Maybe I'm wrong, but that's how I feel. I don't know, I go back and forth on it all the time. I could step back and enjoy myself, but I don't know if retiring would be that enjoyable for me. I've had so much fun doing this job, I don't want to give it up. It's been so good to me, and good for me.

Between the job and Mary Lou and the kids, I've had … really, I've been so lucky in my life. I've made a lot of friends, not too many enemies. It's been … you know … it's been perfect."

The donut shop clears out after the morning rush, and Don looks beleaguered as he glances around the place, void of human activity save for the worker filling the napkin holder.

"This is what I mean," he says, motioning to the empty room. "There's nothing to do. All of a sudden, sitting here … where am I going to go? I always have a place to go when I'm working. I always have somebody to see."

The nicest and luckiest guy in the world may also be the most gregarious. But he was speaking rhetorically.

He knows there are plenty of people to see and places to go if he retires. Don wants to go out on his own terms, and at the moment retirement still sounds too much like waving a white flag. Without a spotlight to share with the local bowlers he would feel like an outsider. The center of the action is where he wants to be. Keeping score, if possible.

But when he finally does get around to kicking back and turning the spotlight on himself for once, he might like what he sees, starting with the 54 years of edifying, reliable sports broadcasts.

He'll take pride in the words of Dan Sharp, who two days after coaching his sixth football state championship at Joliet Catholic quickly returned a phone call to talk about him, saying, "Don Ladas is a good example of how people should live their lives."

He will appreciate that the spiritual footprint he has made includes the sentiments of people like Dick Goss, who wishes "we all could be a little more like him."

Don will enjoy knowing what Kent Irvin said to a guest at the roast: "It's like the line from the movie 'It's A Wonderful Life.' Don is the richest man in town."

He'll be pleased that he's given his wife, children and grandchildren a lifetime of unconditional love, but also that he gave them the best possible gift – a good name, one that will forever be associated with the quiet dignity of having run out every ground ball, having answered every bell, and having done so with a kindness in words that created confidence, a kindness in thought that created profoundness, and a kindness in giving that created love.

Don's exemplary life has enriched a corroding world, and underscored a couple of heartening truths – one being that you can misstep on a perfect game and still go on to have a perfect life, and the other being that sometimes nice guys do finish first.

Printed in the United States
122667LV00002B/199-213/P